The Incredible Eurodollar

The Incredible Eurodollar

W. P. HOGAN
Professor of Economics, University of Sydney

and

I. F. PEARCE
Professor of Economics, University of California (Irvine)

London
GEORGE ALLEN & UNWIN
Boston   Sydney

George Allen & Unwin (Publishers) Ltd,
40 Museum Street, London, WC1A 1LU, UK

George Allen & Unwin (Publishers) Ltd,
Park Lane, Hemel Hempstead, Herts, HP2 4TE, UK

Allen & Unwin Inc.,
9 Winchester Terrace, Winchester, Mass 01890, USA

George Allen & Unwin Australia Pty Ltd,
8 Napier Street, North Sydney, NSW 2060, Australia

First published in 1982

British Library Cataloguing in Publication Data

Hogan, W. P.
    The incredible Eurodollar.
1. Euro-dollar market
I. Title   II. Pearce, I. F.
332.4′5   HG3897
ISBN 0-04-332081-3

Set in 12 on 13 point Garamond by Preface Ltd, Salisbury, Wilts.
and printed in Great Britain by Biddles Ltd, Guildford, Surrey

Contents

4 Eurofinancing in Practice.

5 Market Instability: Risk and Speculation

6 Some Euromarket Folklore

7 Prognosis and Prescription

Acknowledgments

The authors wish to thank numberless friends, and friends of friends in banking and academic circles, who listened patiently to our arguments and enquiries and gave freely of their expertise. Needless to say we accept full responsibility for any errors which may nevertheless remain.

Above all we owe a debt to the University of California at Irvine and to Barbara Sawyer who magically transformed our illegible scrawl into a magnificent manuscript which could only be described as perfect.

Quis Custodiet Ipsos Custodes

'. . . *nobody* really understands the international monetary system . . .' H. Johannes Witteveen — former managing director of the International Monetary Fund and finance minister of the Netherlands.

quoted by 'Adam Smith', *Paper Money* (New York. Summit Books, 1981), p. 109.

1 The Eurodollar Introduced

(i) *An Inevitable Improbability*

Economic events, viewed in retrospect, generate no surprises. Each follows the other in a succession at all times logical, inevitable and predictable. Looking back it is easy to show why that which happened had to happen and why nothing else was ever possible. Looking forward, however, is a very different matter.

Economists of the Middle Ages enjoyed, in some ways, a deeper and more extensive understanding than their modern counterparts of the true and many-sided nature of money. They were able easily to distinguish between 'real' money and 'imaginary' money and indeed explicitly used these terms. It is certain, however, that they could never have thought, even in their most outrageous flights of fancy, that there might one day exist a world, unbelievably more complicated than the one they knew, operating apparently without real money at all. Imaginary money, they would have said, is simply the unit in which real money is measured. The one cannot exist without the other.

Nevertheless it remains true, paradoxically, that, had our learned predecessors actually lived to see the world that was to come, they would have found nothing surprising. The principles remain always the same. The realizations of those principles, on the other hand, exhibit infinite variety leading to unimaginable consequences.

The rise of the Eurodollar market, from very small beginnings some fifteen years ago to a collective institution with monetary assets, almost certainly exceeding in value the annual total of all world international trade put together, is just such a realization. The event was predictable but not predicted, unthinkable beforehand but not surprising ex post facto. At the time of writing it has not reached its full flowering, though we know already that it cannot survive. We do not know what will be the manner of its collapse; or whether indeed it will truly 'collapse', or simply wither away. When it is gone however it will seem obvious why it came about and why it ended as it did.

(ii)   *The Market*

The so-called Eurodollar market is a market in international debt. It accepts deposits and makes loans, which may, in principle, be designated in any currency of any country, provided only that the named currency is sufficiently 'safe' to be internationally acceptable. The named currency would have also to be convertible to other main currencies at exchange rates not subject to too violent or too unpredictable changes. In practice today (1980), the most likely currencies to be designated are US dollars, Sterling, Deutschmarks, Swiss francs, or Japanese yen, with US dollars still the most favored by a very large margin.

Banks that operate in the Eurodollar market are of course, like all banks, highly respectable and respected. Some however are more respectable than others. They range from specially created but independent subsidiaries of major world commercial banks, sometimes operating in the great financial centers and sometimes in small countries with conveniently lenient financial legislation, to so-called 'fringe' banks, called into being by the necessities and opportunities of current world monetary convolutions. All that it is necessary to know at this stage about Eurobanks is that they are able to offer favorable rates of interest on deposits of acceptable currencies and that they are highly experienced in the art of finding borrowers in all parts of the world for all of the funds so deposited. These two facts are of course not unconnected. The one makes possible the other.

It should be understood also that the function of a Eurobank is to underwrite risk. A will not lend to B direct if he does not trust B to repay. But he might very well be happy to deposit funds with a respectable bank, despite the declared intention of that bank to lend to B; for A then enjoys not only B's promise to pay but the bank's promise also if B should default. The likelihood exists a fortiori if A does not know of the bank's lending plans.

Finally it is of crucial importance to emphasize that Eurodollar deposits are *not* checking accounts. They cannot be used to pay bills without first being withdrawn. They are *time* deposits of varying maturities which cannot ordinarily be spent until they are repaid on the due date.

(iii) *What is New?*

The reader might now ask, 'if all this is the case, what is new?' Banks have always accepted deposits and made loans. International loans are commonplace, and have been for many hundreds of years. What is it about the Eurodollar which calls for special explanation?

Part of the answer lies in the astonishing magnitude of current operations, both in absolute size and rate of growth. According to figures published by The Bank for International Settlements (see Chapter 4 below), the total of outstanding Eurodollar deposits amounted, in June 1980, to something of the order of US$ 1,200,000,000,000, which is three to four times the entire money stock of the whole of the USA. More remarkable still is the fact that this total has grown sixfold in eight years, from less than $200 billion in 1972 to the present $1,200 billion in 1980. Furthermore there is every sign that it will have risen between June 1980 and June 1981 by an amount greater than the whole of the *stock* that existed in 1972.

(iv) *Inflation and the Eurodollar*

It is tempting of course to wonder whether the rise of the Eurodollar market is due simply to world inflation or, conversely, whether or not the world inflation is due to the increased 'money' stock now deposited in Eurobanks; but neither of these conjectures bears close examination. There is little correlation between the rise in world prices and the increase in the stock of Eurodollars, nor should we expect there to be. Eurodeposits are not money in the sense that cheques can be drawn upon them. In fact the stock of Eurodollars has risen much faster than the total nominal value of world trade for reasons which need have nothing *directly* to do with inflation.

(v) *Exchange Rates and the Eurodollar*

This does not mean that there is no cause for concern. We have already noticed that the total stock of Eurodollar deposits is today of the same order of magnitude as the annual value of all world trade of all countries put together. This in turn suggests that explicit or implicit transactions in Eurodebt each year might very well equal in value all world commodity trade transactions in the same period. This would be the case if the average maturity time for Eurodollar deposits were twelve months or less as it well might be. Each time a deposit falls due for repayment a decision has to be made whether the debt should be repaid or continued (rolled over) and whether the designated currency should be retained or changed. Debt repayment or roll over may or may not involve the passing of currency across exchanges, but whether it does or not, exchange rates must be affected by the mere fact that the *opportunity* to redesignate the currency exists. Eurobanks deal in currency exchanges and their view of the proper rates must depend as much upon the demand or implied demand for currency to buy and sell debt as upon the demand for currency to buy and sell internationally traded goods.

In the normal way the price of one currency in terms of another (the exchange rate) will settle so as to equate the supply and demand for traded commodities, that is, to balance trade. But if at the same time there is a demand to change the currency designation of significant quantities of maturing debt, according to expectations of future exchange rate changes based upon extrapolation of past observations or other cause, then it seems likely that a free market in currencies will fail in its primary function, namely, to balance trade. The existence of the Eurodollar market may very well serve to sustain the very forces which cause the Eurodollar market to grow. This is a classical case of economic instability.

(vi) *The Eurodollar Market and Risk*

More important still is the risk of chaos, of more than one kind, which could be brought about by major default on Euro-debt. The figures quoted above viewed as debt are not especially disturbing. It is everywhere agreed, of course, that there is no way in which existing liabilities could be repaid by the borrowers, except over a very long period of time, and that even long-term repayment would hardly be possible in the present political climate. On the other hand, it is quite usual for an individual to borrow two or even three times his annual income, and few countries have, as yet, taken on international debt of this order of magnitude. These considerations have led some commentators to ask why repayment need ever be attempted. After all, governments do not usually see it as their duty to repay national debt, only to pay the interest.

There are a number of answers to this. It is true that we would think it normal for a person to borrow three times his annual income to buy, say, his home; but no credit company would agree to lend three years' purchasing power to buy non-durable consumer goods. The reason is simple. A home can always be sold to repay debt but that which is already consumed cannot be sold. Consumer credit can be repaid only out of income. Banks which might be willing to lend money to individuals to buy housing would almost certainly be unwilling to lend to the same individual to buy whiskey. But the very same bank will often lend money to governments to finance a trade deficit whether or not that trade deficit was generated by the overpurchase of building materials or whiskey.

There is, unfortunately, considerable evidence to suggest that the deficits of some countries are indeed induced by unwise overconsumption. It is *not* true that all international borrowing is matched by a corresponding accumulation of real capital in the borrowing country, implying an increase in its capacity to pay interest appropriately. The reason for this lies quite simply in the fact that governments and/or central banks are frequently the principal borrowers. Neither governments nor central banks are ordinarily required to deposit collateral, particularly when their borrowings are apparently required only to support exchange rates in accordance with international agreements. It is not usual to doubt the capacity to repay of official borrowers if only because of a universal belief that someone, somehow, is bound to come to the rescue of official borrowers in a crisis. This attitude has been reinforced one hundredfold in recent years by the establishment and growth of international institutions and agreements precisely designed to rescue official debtors whenever they are too much embarrassed. One of the great myths of our time finds expression in the universal belief that no kind of economic activity should ever be inhibited by lack of money. The necessity to limit spending to the level of one's capacity to pay has been translated by experts to mean a 'lack of liquidity', easily treated by the creation of credit. Accordingly the automatic mechanism which ordinarily serves to correct imbalances of trade has been replaced by a mechanism which automatically produces the credit needed to sustain unlimited imbalances. Lip service only is paid to the inescapable need for countries to face the facts of life.

(vii)   *How Much Debt is Tolerable?*

Debt may be tolerable but whether it is or not depends upon its magnitude. Growing debt not matched by capital growth sooner or later becomes intolerable as interest charges absorb a growing proportion of the national product. When it does become intolerable debt must be repudiated. What, therefore, is disturbing about Eurodollar debt is, above all else, its 25 percent annual rate of growth. Eurodebt is growing faster than world inflation and much faster than the capacity of debtor nations to pay the growing service charges.

We comment finally in this section upon two further matters of fact. First, it is already clear that banks operating in the Eurodollar market are themselves anxious over possible default. More and more they are creating lending consortia in the belief that this will somehow lessen the risks of which they are conscious. There exists an increasing awareness that it is not just a question of whether the whole structure is sound. Rather it is a question whether part of it is unsound. The repudiation of a relatively small debt which is unsound could lead to a progressive attempt to withdraw even those deposits which are quite safely invested. A large proportion of Eurodollar deposits are short term. It is a matter of concern what might happen if repayment of short-term deposits on a large scale were demanded because of a loss of confidence either in the designated currency or in the likelihood of ultimate repayment by borrowers.

Second, it is the case that significant defaults have already been observed. More than one borrowing country has had its Eurodebt 'restructured', which is the euphemistic term for 'partially written off'. The argument that some default is inevitable is reinforced by the observation that some degree of default has already been observed.

(viii) *Who is Liable?*

Of course nobody minds too much, apart from a limited number of creditors, when a borrower defaults. After all lenders are rich and borrowers are poor! The distribution of income does not begin by being 'fair'. There is nothing new in the repudiation of debt, nor are its consequences necessarily wholly bad. In the case of the Eurodollar market, however, there is an important feature which is new, if not in principle at least in its order of importance.

If a loan is made through the good offices of a financial intermediary then that financial institution is liable for the debt as well as the defaulting debtor. It is possible therefore that a Eurobank might find itself in trouble as well as the original debtor. Indeed it could be, and sometimes is, argued quite falsely that dollar debt can come into being only because US citizens import more than they export, and hence that all such debt is ultimately a US liability. This is of course not the case.

The falsity of the argument does not, on the other hand, alter the fact that the first line of defence of any Eurobank short of money may well, in practice, be the Eurodollar market as a whole. In a general way it is possible, at very short notice, to borrow very large sums of money in the Eurodollar market, sufficient for a single bank to secure all the liquidity it needs to handle minor crises. Nor in the case of a major crisis would it matter if a single bank collapsed. There is nothing new in this.

What is new is the extent and complexity of the links which any failing bank will almost certainly have, directly or indirectly, with the central bank in some major financial center. Suppose, for example, that a British subsidiary of an English clearing bank, operating in the Eurodollar market, stood in danger of failure because of a loan default on the US dollar designated debt of some country located, say, in South America. Suppose further that the Eurobank concerned was physically located in the Cayman Islands and had advanced dollars to South America, originally deposited by an oil producing country in the Middle East. When the Eurobank fails, must the parent bank in the UK meet the debt when it had no hand in negotiating it? And if the parent bank is liable and if it too fails in consequence may it then appeal to the Bank of England as lender of last resort? And if the currency required is US dollars and the Bank of England has insufficient US dollars in its reserves can it then appeal to the US Federal Reserve System for help under gentleman's agreements made for quite a different purpose than that of underwriting trade debts between two countries which have nothing to do with either the USA *or* the UK? Where does responsibility end? Is the USA after all responsible for debts of non-nationals just because they happened to be designated in US dollars?

(ix) *Is the System Understood?*

Much more serious than anything so far mentioned is the possibility that some implications of the Eurodollar market might not be properly understood either by some who operate in that market or by all whose responsibility it should be to secure a proper environment for efficient economic activity in general.

In particular, the fact that international indebtedness in recent times commonly takes the form of bank deposits and loans, rather than the more familiar nineteenth century government bonds sold direct to private investors overseas, invites modern monetary experts to classify Eurodeposits as 'money' rather than 'debt'. Monetary theory today customarily includes time deposits in its 'M3' measure of the money stock, and many governments think it is more important to control the quantity of M3 than M1. Accordingly we find in the banking literature expressions of concern as to whether a dollar deposit in a Swiss bank should be counted as part of the money stock of Switzerland, the USA or even Turkey to whom the deposit was onlent to buy, shall we say, wool from Australia. The deposit in the Swiss bank and the corresponding loan to Turkey remain obstinately recorded in the Eurobank books even though the actual dollars have by now returned to the USA after being used by Australians to buy Virginian tobacco.

The propensity to count Eurodollar deposits as money has led to many curious propositions. It has been supposed that somehow Eurodollar operations create new dollars outside of the control of US authorities, thereby increasing the world stock of acceptable money with inflationary implications. Even those who understand that debt is not spendable wealth until someone, willing to save, can be found to buy that debt, frequently take the view that somehow the Eurodollar market raises the velocity of circulation of money and so is inflationary.

At the same time the very considerable literature on the Eurodollar market reveals wide differences of opinion on the very first question, 'how does the debt arise and why does it grow so fast?' Because much of the debt is designated in US dollars it has been thought that the underlying cause must be US trade deficits. But published figures show that, against the total of Eurodeposits, the total of all US trade deficits is microscopic. Other writers have claimed that, by the normal application of fractional reserve banking, the total of US trade deficits can be 'multiplied' to create deposits far in excess of the original deficits and that this is the underlying explanation.

These misconceptions have given rise to proposals echoed by the highest state officials, which, if the object is to check the growth of the market, could not possibly succeed.

It has been suggested, for example, that Eurobanks should be required to hold dollar deposits (i.e. reserves) in US banks equal to some fixed proportion of their total loans. But this would do nothing to check the inflow of funds. It would simply change the form in which Eurobanks hold their assets, raising the ratio of cash to loans. At the same time it would invite participating banks to devise new and even more ingenious ways to flout unnecessary international regulations, leaving the underlying causes of the problem untouched.

(x)   *The Heart of the Matter*

The truth is that the Eurodollar market came into being because of a tendency for the *same* countries always to be in trade surplus and the *same* countries always to be in trade deficit. It is not the US trade deficit which creates the debt but the accumulated trade imbalances of the whole world. The market will exist as long as the debt exists and will not go away until it is funded or until those countries, now in trade surplus, engineer a deficit and those in deficit engineer a surplus. In other words we have to reestablish the mechanism which automatically balances real trade and abolish the newly discovered liquidity-creating machinery, artificial and evolutionary, which, because it 'recycles' funds which have already been spent so that they might be spent again, so much excites the admiration of politicians who wish to give away more than the countries they govern are able to produce.

It is the purpose of the following chapters to defend more satisfactorily some of the assertions made above. The method in Chapters 2 and 3 will be to trace, in a hypothetical world, events that we should expect logically to occur in given circumstances and hence, by implication, to examine their likeness to those happenings which we see around us. Later we shall describe in some detail the present state and some of the current practices of the Euromarket, and comment at greater length on particular proposals for its reform.

2 Why It All Happened

(i) *Balance of Trade Identities*

Regrettably it is impossible to understand fully the Eurodollar market without first understanding some of the principles of international trade. More regrettably still the principles of international trade are far from easy to comprehend and are seldom well presented in text books. The most common introductions to the subject differ markedly from anything that could be said even to approach the whole of the relevant truth and in some cases manifestly false arguments have been widely disseminated.

A good beginning can be made with a plain, almost trivial, statement of fact. 'Goods which the people of any country consume must be produced at home or imported from abroad. There exists no other source of supply.' This not very profound observation leads to a fundamental proposition from which very deep conclusions follow. It *must* be the case that, in any time period for any country,

$$\text{Consumption} = \text{Production plus Imports less Exports} \quad (1)$$

By 'consumption' is meant everything that is purchased including both capital goods and consumer goods, whether used in production or in the pursuit of pleasure or welfare.

In claiming that the fundamental identity (1) above *must* hold at all times we do of course imply that unwanted stocks (inventories) do not exist. To be more precise we ought to have written,

$$\text{Consumption plus Unintended Additions to Stocks} = \text{Production plus Imports less Exports} \quad (2)$$

Unwanted additions to stocks are, of course, an indication of a breakdown or temporary failure of the market-price mechanism to equate supply and demand. Alternatively, it could be argued that unwanted stocks will always be observed *before* the market has had time to make the necessary adjustments to the most recent disturbance, that is, the market may be working but the process takes time.

Bearing in mind the identity (2) consider now the consequences of consuming, in the broad sense of both capital and utility-creating goods, at all times just exactly the value of goods produced. This is the same as never being a net borrower or lender. We could then deduce from the identity (2) above that

Imports less Exports = Balance of Trade =
    Unwanted Additions to Stocks   (3)

In other words there could be no imbalance of trade unless at the same time at least one goods market is somewhere failing to clear. Supply would have to be different from demand.

Equations (1) and (3) represent two different views of trade imbalance which can be greatly at variance with more simplistic accounts of the relationship between exchange rates and the level of trade. It is not true that currency depreciation will always, or even usually, correct a trade imbalance simply by raising import prices in the home market and by reducing export prices in the foreign market. Indeed, if an observed trade imbalance is due to an excess of production over aggregate consumption, whether or not markets are cleared, no amount of exchange rate adjustment, by itself, can ever correct that imbalance. Price changes, whether engineered by currency depreciation or not, cannot ordinarily do more than equate supply and demand. They cannot at the same time ensure that total consumption is restricted to the value of production. And when consumption is different from production trade *cannot*, by the identity (1) above, be balanced, even though markets are everywhere cleared. The belief that price changes alone can, and did, correct trade imbalances was not unreasonable in the nineteenth century. It is not however appropriate to modern times.

A particularly sad feature of economic life is that, no sooner have we collectively achieved some degree of understanding of cause and effect, than circumstances change so radically that the painfully acquired knowledge is already out of date. In particular is this true of the problem of the balance of payments.

(ii)   *The Balance of Payments in the Past*

In the nineteenth century it was taken for granted the governments must properly balance their budgets and that all countries should live within their means, that is, money should not be created out of nothing, unsupported by equivalent production. In these circumstances production and consumption *had* to be broadly equal.

The rules of the game were not, of course, always obeyed. But they were obeyed sufficiently well to make it reasonable for economists to develop their theories on the *assumption* that they were always obeyed. Observed trade imbalances were relatively small and seldom persistent.* They arose, usually, because markets failed to clear. Explicit and clearly understood bilateral loans excepted, countries did not overspend, so that an observed imbalance of payments for any country was matched by an accumulation of unwanted stocks within that country. Economists perceived no need to enquire what policy should be applied to correct an imbalance; for they knew that no policy was called for. They sought only to show how the automatic mechanism worked and to prove its stability. They asked only whether corrective forces pulled or pushed in the right direction. Did exchanges adjust so as to equate the

---

*Alfred Marshall (1923) felt it quite proper to write, for example, 'The trade of a country is taken to consist of her exports of goods on the one side and her import of goods on the other: *and the aggregate value of these two groups tends to be equal.*'

supply and demand for currencies? Did specie movements, the direct consequence of payments imbalance, lead automatically to price changes calculated to remove the imbalance or to enlarge it?

The conclusions reached were that markets were for the most part stable. Although it was known that unstable cases could be constructed, instability was not considered to be important in practice. Those views were justified both by the facts and by the arguments. The correcting mechanism, as it was then understood, operated purely through price, with or without exchange rate changes, in the following manner.

As long as production equaled consumption imports could be greater than exports in value if, and only if, unplanned stocks were rising. Unplanned stock accumulation could be of export goods, importable goods and/or of goods and services that were excluded from trade by prohibitive transport costs (non-traded goods). At the same time the excess of imports over exports would give rise to an excess home demand for foreign currency over supply.

In the case where the home currency was made up of bank notes or home bank deposits not acceptable abroad in payment of debts, the trade imbalance would naturally generate a change in the rate of exchange, that is, a rise in the price of foreign currency in terms of home currency. There would be an excess of home demand for foreign currency over supply earned by exports. This would:

(1) make exports easier and/or more profitable to sell abroad by widening the gap between home costs of production and foreign market price expressed in home currency;

(2) discourage imports by narrowing the profit gap between home market prices and foreign purchase prices expressed in home currency;

(3) induce a switch of home consumption from traded to non-traded goods by the rise in the home price of traded goods relative to non-traded goods likely to follow (1) and (2) above.

Clearly the mechanisms (1), (2) and (3), together or separately, must have served to check the growth of unplanned stocks in the home country wherever they occurred. The imbalance of payments would have been automatically corrected and with it the excess demand for foreign currency.

In cases where home and foreign currencies consisted solely of gold or silver coinage with intrinsic worth, or whenever a paper currency embodied a credible promise to redeem notes with bullion on demand, currency exchange rates could not vary significantly. However, the price mechanism worked in a very similar way to that described above.

A bullion or bullion-backed currency differs from a pure paper currency in that it is readily acceptable in payment of debts in any country as if it were bullion. Foreign currency need not be bought to finance import surpluses since foreign payments could always be made in bullion or bullion equivalent. If any country was experiencing a trade deficit it would be losing bullion abroad, inducing a home scarcity of bullion and a rise in its price. The average price of all goods at home would be falling relative to bullion and the average price of all goods abroad rising, the more especially because of the presence of unwanted stocks. It is easy to see that this is equivalent to a currency depreciation and would have precisely the effects (1), (2) and (3) listed above.

This brief account of what might be called 'old-fashioned' balance of payments adjustment theory has been presented not because it is relevant to what follows but because it is necessary to draw attention to its irrelevance. What is important today is not the price mechanism. Rather it is the widespread introduction, in recent times, of government *policies* which in fact interfere with the price mechanism. To see this it is convenient to reverse the nineteenth century view and to imagine a world where it is taken for granted that markets are always cleared. We need to pay more attention to the relationship between production and consumption than to the price mechanism equating the supply and demand for goods. This point of view is developed further in the next section.

(iii)   *The Balance of Payments in the Mid-Twentieth Century*

We have already drawn attention, in Chapter 1, to the principal axiom of the conventional wisdom of the immediate past, which held it to be the case that all unwanted stocks are unambiguously bad and that the evil of unwanted stocks exists only because of a shortage of money, easily remedied by the creation of credit. It is true, of course, that sometimes, perhaps often, unwanted stocks have provoked businessmen into believing that they should reduce production and use their cash flow to extinguish their debt, thereby creating periods of serious involuntary unemployment. It is true also that unemployment, like inflation and even more so a declining general price level, occasions great distress. But it is a mistake of monumental proportions, in consequence of that distress, to ignore completely the part played by the existence of unwanted stocks in the signaling process which imposes upon individuals unpleasant pressures requiring them to respond as producers to their own demands as consumers.

No one disputes that goods or labor offered for sale but remaining unsold create a problem. Nor is it denied that the immediate problem could almost certainly be treated at once by creating and distributing money, given that money can be brought into being without cost. But in such a case we jump out of the frying pan only to end up in the fire.

Production creates income and income is always spent; for those who do not spend their incomes lend what they have not spent to those who will. Newly created money therefore, put into the hands of consumers, ensures that an *attempt* will be made to spend more than the value of goods created, whether there is unemployment or not. This does not mean, of course, that, ex post facto, the community necessarily will have *succeeded* in consuming more than the value of its production; for the consequence might simply be that prices rise until the market value of goods produced is equal to incomes earned in the previous period plus the value of the printed money. If, on the other hand, the country does succeed in consuming (at the resulting market price) more than the value of its product (at the same market prices) this must be because it has succeeded in importing more in value terms than it was able to export. In other words the creation of paper money or credit designed to stimulate consumer demand *necessarily* results either in an excess of imports over exports, a balance of trade problem, or inflation, or a little of both. Furthermore it inhibits and can entirely destroy the price mechanism that would otherwise communicate the needs of consumers to the producers of goods. The fire is much hotter than the frying pan.

Unwanted stocks arise not because there is insufficient demand, in the aggregate, to buy at constant prices all that is produced, but because, given prices, the wrong things have been produced, or because the international terms of trade are 'wrong' so that too great a proportion of aggregate demand is directed abroad. To print and spend money in these circumstances may equate supply and demand in the home market but only at the cost of overriding the signal to producers and price setters indicating a need for change. One problem is solved at the cost of introducing new problems much more serious than that just escaped; for the market problem would have gone away by itself while the new problems will not. The mechanisms (1), (2) and (3) of p. 15 above are switched off by the printed money. It is not the case that government policies are needed because markets do not work. Rather it is that government policies do not work because markets do. The fact is that for *every* level of government money printing there exists a different set of prices that will clear markets, whatever the exchange rate; and a *different* imbalance of payments to be supported by IMF handouts or Eurodollar 'recycling' corresponds to each set of prices.

These claims, in all their tedious detail, will be substantiated in the next several sections.

(iv)   *A Multiple 'Equilibrium' Diagram*

Both supply and demand are much more responsive to price changes in a large catchment area than a small one simply because there are more persons to respond. Market adjustment in the larger area is achieved by quantity changes rather than price changes. It is not unreasonable to suppose therefore that the relative prices of traded goods throughout the world are much more stable and common to all countries than the relative price of traded goods to non-traded goods within each single country. For the one, the whole world is the market; for the other, by definition, the market exists only in each single country. Furthermore, if a single country is experiencing a trade deficit because it is consuming too much, then the rest of the world must be consuming less than the value of its product by the same amount. That is to say, whenever one country has a trade deficit the rest of the world must have a corresponding surplus. By definition, therefore, the impact of a trade deficit must fall almost entirely on non-traded goods within the country developing the deficit; for *total* world demand for all goods is unaffected by trade deficits or surpluses, being equal always to total world production. Demand for traded goods within each country is affected only by differences in national likes and dislikes which make themselves felt only when one country increases its consumption of traded goods at the expense of other countries, thereby creating a trade deficit. On the other hand, if a single country consumes less, then there must be a fall in aggregate demand for its non-traded goods since, by definition, persons in other countries now consuming more do not buy the non-traded goods of any country but their own.

These considerations make it possible to develop the argument below, with a much simplified model. It is convenient and justifiable to suppose that the *relative* prices of all traded goods throughout the world remain given and fixed. The only *relative* price changes which need be considered are those within countries between traded and non-traded goods.

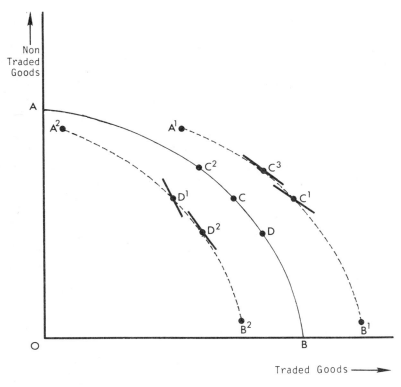

Figure 1   *Diagram illustrating multiple equilibrium possibilities.*

In the diagram presented in Figure 1 the vertical axis OA measures non-traded goods and the axis OB traded goods. The boundary AB defines the complete inventory of combinations of traded and non-traded goods that might be made available for consumption in a given country by making the best possible use, both in trade and production, of that country's limited resources. The point C, for example, indicates that, for a given quantity of non-traded goods produced, as measured by the vertical distance of C from OB, the horizontal distance of C from OA is the maximum quantity of traded goods that the country can acquire by production and/or exchange. Each point in the set of points bounded by AB and the axes OA and

OB defines a pair of quantities of traded and non-traded goods that might be consumed. The whole set might be termed therefore the 'consumption possibility set'. On the other hand, it would obviously be inefficient to market and sell any pair of quantities not on the boundary AB since, for any other point, it would always be possible to have more of both commodities. Competition ensures efficiency so that only AB is relevant.

Because only points on the boundary are efficient we are able to deduce also that the slope of the boundary curve at each point measures the relative costs of production of traded and non-traded goods; for if we change production from, say, C to D, the slope of the straight line between C and D indicates what quantity of non-traded goods must be given up in exchange for traded goods to achieve the 'consumption possibility' D. And since the same resources are able to produce both C or D the non-traded goods given up must be equal in cost to the extra traded goods made available. The ratio of goods exchanged therefore measures the cost of a unit of one measured in units of the other, which is the same as the ratio of their money costs of production. The closer the points C and D the more the straight line CD approximates to the slope of the boundary AB.

Notice also that, given the assumption that the ratios of all prices of traded goods are fixed throughout the world, we do not have to consider trade at all. The effects of international trading activities, with *balanced trade*, are embodied in the shape of the boundary curve AB. It does not matter what class of traded goods is actually produced by the home country. It is possible always to consume any bundle of traded goods of the same value, simply by exchanging what is produced at home with the rest of the world according to need. The assumption that the consumption possibility set includes *all* possible points implies that in constructing the boundary AB, the country concerned would be supposed to produce and exchange those traded goods it could manufacture most cheaply so as to maximise the total value of traded goods available to it. The cost of production of a traded good, as measured by the slope of AB, means the cost of production of that class of traded good which can be manufactured with least resources. Any profit earned by producers of traded goods includes the profit on trade as well as on production.

Finally it should be understood that the particular shape of the boundary curve AB, as drawn in the diagram, reflects the fact that, as more non-traded goods and fewer traded goods are manufactured, the cost of producing non-traded goods *rises* relatively. More traded goods must be given up for each extra unit of non-traded goods produced. This accords with observation and theory. Conversely, as more non-traded goods are offered for sale in the country represented in the diagram their market price must fall relatively. The point C should be taken to be the point where the cost of producing both classes of goods, including normal profits, just equals the market price. 'Normal' profits means that the same rate of profit per unit of money capital employed is earned in all activities.

The first crucial point can now be made. Because, moving around the curve AB from A to B, the cost of producing traded goods is rising continuously relative to non-traded goods, and because, at the same time, the market price of traded goods must be continuously falling relative to non-traded goods, the point C where relative cost and price ratios are equal *is unique*. At one and only one point on AB, namely, C, can cost, including profit, be equal to market price for both traded and non-traded goods.

The second crucial point to note is that C, where supply equals demand at prices equal to cost, is the only possible pattern of consumption on AB, for the country represented, which allows its foreign trade to be in balance. Only at C will markets be cleared when the price charged is equal to cost. At the same time, when C is both made available by production and actually consumed, the value of consumption must be the same as the value of production. Accordingly, by the identity (2) (p. 12), trade must be balanced. Any other pattern of expenditure, whether on AB or not, necessarily implies either uncleared markets or, in the case where the bundle of goods consumed does not lie on AB, consumption different from production.

Now suppose that, for reasons to be considered in detail later, production and imports paid for by goods exported generate the supply of goods C, but the value of consumption exceeds the value of production. If the country depicted in the diagram is successful in its excess consumption this must be because it has managed to buy abroad more traded goods than it was able to produce or obtain by exchange *with balanced trade*. It must have been able in fact to persuade the rest of the world to give traded goods for money instead of for traded goods of a different class. The consumption point can be outside the consumption possibility boundary because traded goods can be bought with money as well as produced and/or bought with goods. The consumption pattern of the home country will have moved from C to C^1, a point to the right but on the same level as C. C^1 *must* be on the same level since there is no way that any country can consume more non-traded goods than it produces itself. In short the possibility now entertained of buying, with money, goods equal in quantity to the distance between C^1 and C shifts the whole consumption possibility set AB to the right to A^1B^1. The horizontal distance between AB and A^1B^1 and the slopes of the two curves (given the same quantity of non-traded goods) remain the same.

Notice now that prices that served to clear markets at C are not likely to be those that would clear the market at C^1; for if there are more traded goods for sale with the same amount of non-traded goods then the price of traded goods would be expected to have to fall relatively. It would become profitable to produce more non-traded goods and fewer traded goods. The 'production' point C would move towards A around AB. This implies that the consumption point C^1 must move in step in such a way as to remain to the right and on the same level as C as it moves, that is, it must move around A^1B^1, given a constant level of exchange of traded goods for money. The consumption of non-traded goods must always remain equal to home production.

As the consumption of non-traded goods rises relative to the consumption of traded goods, prices required to clear the market must change. Traded goods become more expensive relative to non-traded goods. At the same time, as production C moves towards A, the cost of *producing* traded goods gets smaller relative to the cost of producing non-traded goods. Fewer non-traded goods need be given up to secure one unit of traded goods. It follows that some point on AB, between C and A (say C^2), must exist where the relative market clearing prices for the corresponding pattern of consumption (say C^3) on A^1B^1 are the same as the relative costs of production at C^2.

As an aid to understanding short unbroken lines have been drawn on the diagram through C^3 and C^1, the slopes of which indicate market clearing price ratios consistent with the argument above.

The main point should now be clear. If a country is producing at C^2 and consuming at C^3 there need be no involuntary stock changes. Supply equals demand everywhere. All markets are cleared but consumption exceeds production and there is a corresponding imbalance of trade. As long as the country concerned can continue to persuade the rest of the world to take its money rather than its goods there is no mechanism that will eliminate the imbalance. The only tricks that need to be performed to permit indefinite overconsumption and permanent imbalance are the tricks with money, which will be considered later. Before we turn to this however two further points must be emphasized.

(v) *Multiple 'Equilibrium' – World Markets Cleared*

First it must be understood that C^2 is *not* unique. C *is* a unique equilibrium because it is the only pattern of consumption that is consistent with cleared markets *and* zero excess consumption, that is, balanced trade. As soon, however, as excess consumption is permitted, there can be seen to be any number of possibilities consistent with cleared markets. For each different level of consumption of traded goods imported and paid for in money rather than goods there is a different curve like A^1B^1 lying outside the original consumption possibility set. And for each curve like A^1B^1 there is a point like C^3 where markets are cleared at prices equal to production costs plus normal profits.

Second, it is necessary to draw attention to the position of the rest of the trading world. Suppose that the diagram now represents the rest of the world instead of the home country. Suppose further that for some reason, as explained in the next section, the rest of the world consumes *less* than the value of its production, C. The pattern of consumption would have to be represented by some point D^1 to the left of production C implying, as in the home country, an unchanged consumption of non-traded goods despite the fact that total *consumption* is by assumption less than total production. This time at D^1 the market-clearing price of non-traded goods would be below cost making it profitable to switch production to traded goods. At some point, D^2, market-clearing prices would be the same as production costs at D. Given a 'fixed' quantity of traded goods exported by the rest of the world to the home country for money rather than goods, the relevant consumption possibility line A^2B^2 lies inside the boundary AB of the original consumption possibility set. Consumption must settle at D^2 and production at D where relative costs are the same as relative market-clearing prices. Supply and demand would be equated with no problems except that of the willingness of the rest of the world to accept money from the home country in exchange for goods.

Clearly the overconsumption of the home country must exactly match the underconsumption of the rest of the world, a fact reflected in the diagram by the equality of the horizontal distances between A^2B^2 and AB and between AB and A^1B^1. This equality must hold even though the home country and the rest of the world should properly have been represented with separate and widely different consumption possibility sets. Nothing indeed could be more obvious than that, if all markets are cleared, the successful consumption, ex post facto, of the home country must be equal to the failure to consume, ex post facto, of the rest of the world. The only source of goods is world production. If one country consumes others can not. Total world supply equals total world demand by the fact that inventories remain unchanged.

(vi) *Multiple 'Equilibrium' and the Market Mechanism — Excess Consumption by Forgery*

We wish especially to emphasize in this section a point already made, namely, that when there are many different 'final positions' where world supply equals world demand and many different ways in which prices might adjust, it is more likely that supply will everywhere equal demand than that it will not. In the previous section the existence of many 'final positions' was established. It is necessary now to consider the equally many routes by which any one of the 'final positions' might be attained.

We begin, as usual, with what used to be rather than what is, not because it is especially relevant but to point up the contrast. In the nineteenth century excess spending over production was not, of course, entirely unknown. The straightforward way in which a country might succeed in consuming more than the value of its product would be for individuals within that country, or its government, to borrow money from the rest of the world. If the borrowed money is to be successfully spent, without raising prices, extra goods must be bought from abroad. Imports would have to exceed exports (assuming cleared markets), the excess being paid for with the borrowed money.

Notice that the process builds up debt. Borrowing means selling bonds. Sensible borrowing means selling long-term bonds which can be sold if necessary by the holder to a third party should he need his money back. The third party has to be brought in if the borrower has borrowed to spend as he usually has; for the borrower having spent cannot pay back except out of his current income. The bonds sold by the borrower are not money since they cannot be spent without saving by some third person who is prepared to buy existing bonds from the original lender now wishing to spend what he originally saved.

All this describes the process whereby the British people in the nineteenth century financed, shall we say, the development of Argentine railways. Markets were cleared everywhere. Britain enjoyed an export surplus and the Argentine suffered a deficit paid for by the sale of bonds. There was no balance of *payments* problem only an imbalance of trade. International debt grew just as it does today in the Eurodollar market; but the lenders knew to whom they were lending and were able to judge the risk. Furthermore the debt was long term and not bank underwritten. In no way could the lender demand repayment at short notice. No one believed that extra money was being created, nor was it. No one thought the lending to be inflationary, nor was it. Nor could the lending exceed what the British people were prepared to save or have their government raise in taxes.

Of course, as explained in the previous section, the underspending by Britain and the overspending in the Argentine must have generated the relative price changes necessary to clear markets. The price of non-traded goods must have fallen relatively in the UK and risen relatively in the Argentine, provided, that is, that no offsetting trading relationship with some third country had introduced a further complication.

How might the necessary price changes have come about? What should have happened, and what probably did, is very simple and sensible. The money lent to the Argentine must sooner or later, directly or indirectly have been spent back in the UK; for if supply equals demand everywhere, the country not spending the value of its product, UK, is the only country where goods are available not matched by demand. What is likely however is that the consumer goods that British savers would have bought if they had not saved would have been different in kind from the capital goods that Argentinian borrowers were seeking. At first unwanted stocks and excess demands must have appeared. But prices would have adjusted to this, generating changes in the pattern of supply until world markets were cleared. Individuals, and producers, respond under pressure to signals generated by their own demands as consumers.

All of this is as it should be. Indeed there is a powerful sense in which the new equilibrium, after the borrowing, *was unique*, as it would have been if there had been no international borrowing. Individuals in the UK consciously made up their minds to save a certain proportion of their income determined by their own wishes. They further decided to buy assets in the Argentine. They knew what they were buying and assessed the risks. It could even be said that UK spending did *not* after all fall short of the value of the UK product. The view might be taken that the Argentine actually and deliberately exported rights to income derived from its capital assets equal in value to its (apparent) excess imports of goods. Conversely the UK knowingly bought rights to Argentine income which did not appear among 'visible' imports. What appeared to be excess consumption in the Argentine might be interpreted as neither arbitrary nor excess but as paid for by the sale of future income following an act of deliberate and well considered choice, no different from any other sale or purchase. Observed trade might appear out of balance but virtual trade need not be.

The problem of the twentieth century is quite different. If nineteenth century governments had believed, as twentieth century governments do, that the 'hidden hand' of Adam Smith was in desperate need of guidance, they might have behaved in quite a different way. Britain, for example, observing its unwanted stocks of consumer goods, might have thought it proper to print money to 'spend its way out of the slump'. Alternatively the Bank of England, noting an apparent reduction in the domestically held money stock or a rise in interest rates, and being under instruction to 'control' the supply of money, might very well, as an act of policy, have bought government bonds with newly created money. Former owners of government bonds would then have had new money to lend making possible that much more spending. In the jargon of the 1930s the outflow of money to the Argentine might have been 'sterilized'. This behavior opens a whole new range of possibilities.

Efforts, based on money manipulation, to deflect the hidden hand do nothing to influence the final real equilibrium. But they do influence the path to equilibrium; and, by the same token, *persistent* monetary 'guidance' applied to the hidden hand can prevent the attainment of long-run equilibrium indefinitely. True 'sterilization' of monetary outflows cannot really be secured by creating more money. All that can be secured by creating money, unmatched by production, is inflation. Money lent abroad does not disappear. It passes from hand to hand until, one fine day, it arrives back in the country it started from in search of the goods already sold to the happy recipients of the new money created to replace it when it left. It is not surprising that we live today in a generally inflation-ridden world. Nor is it surprising that inflation should play a part in the new trade-price-adjustment mechanism. Account must be taken of this.

The twentieth-century differs also from the nineteenth century in another important respect. Probably, for the first time in the whole of its history, the world presently finds itself without any kind of money at all, possessed of intrinsic value either in the form of commodity money or of pledges to redeem notes for valuable goods. Real money has faded away, the last vestige disappearing in 1973, when the USA abandoned finally all that was left of its promise in certain circumstances to pay gold for dollars on demand. There exists, currently, no standard of value anywhere on earth. Forward contracts are entered into with some knowledge of what they mean at the moment of signing but with little knowledge of what they will mean the day after, beyond a set of expectations based more upon hope than upon any knowledge of economic theory or fact.

In the nineteenth century, rates of exchange between national currencies could not vary significantly from those determined by the bullion content of the coinage or whatever promise to pay was embodied in the note issue. Today we have so-called 'market-determined' exchange rates which are not in fact market-determined.

Market-determined exchange rates sound appealing to a generation just now rediscovering the value of markets. We may, however, have overlooked the fact that a market in currencies not possessed of intrinsic value is a contradiction in terms. The rate at which goods (or monies) exchange in a true market are determined by their intrinsic value. If they have no value there can be no real market. Coins in the Middle Ages exchanged by and large according to their bullion content precisely because there *was* a market. Efforts to maintain the exchange value of debased coinage by decree failed, not because there was an excess supply of debased coinage, but because there existed a market in bullion and because all of the people cannot be fooled all of the time.

The paragraphs above should not be read as an argument for the restoration of a bullion standard. This is clearly both impossible and undesirable today. Nor should it be read as an argument for a new kind of money although a new kind of 'proper' money in some form is bound to come in due course. All that is hoped for is that the reader will accept a simple point. Freely fluctuating exchange rates, when they really do fluctuate, are simply the inevitable consequence of the license to print money granted to governments and/or banks by the introduction of money which costs nothing to create. It is just not possible to have stable exchange rates *and* at the same time to use the supply of money as an instrument of policy. Fluctuating exchange rates do not determine the relative price of currencies. All that they do is to reflect the current price of goods and/or debt (see below) in the various countries concerned, which prices are in turn determined by the amount of money put into circulation by home governments and banks.

Printing money redistributes real income in favor of the printer by raising prices; not by an infinite amount against the forger and by nothing at all against the holder of proper money, as it should be, but equally against everyone. Printing money, therefore, is truly a policy as long as it continues. When it ceases values return to what they were. The real equilibrium reestablishes itself. If we make the mistake, as we have done, of supposing that exchange rates ought to remain constant even though we indiscriminately print money *a redistribution of income can take place between countries even though the forgeries occur only in one country*. The redistribution so achieved can affect the balance of payments, for as long as forgery continues, just as if there were genuine nineteenth century lending.

Reconsider the case of Britain and the Argentine in the nineteenth century given today's conventional wisdom. Suppose that Argentina, impelled by a Keynes-like philosophy, had thought it better to finance her railway construction with printed money. Suppose further that Britain, delighted to export and receive foreign currency reserves, had expressed herself willing to accept payment for real capital exports in Argentine currency. Somehow the Bank of England would then have been required to find the sterling counterpart of the Argentine money to complete the payment to British exporters. The proper thing to do, if the Bank were determined to hold the Argentine money in reserve, would have been to sell securities in exchange for sterling, thereby imposing forced saving upon the British people equivalent to the excess spending in the Argentine. If goods prices adjusted accordingly so as to clear markets the only difference between this and the nineteenth century transaction described above would have been that the British act of saving was imposed by Bank of England policy rather than by free choice on the part of individuals, all in reaction to the Argentine initiative.

Suppose, on the other hand, that the Bank of England had not raised the required sterling by the sale of securities but simply printed it, buying with the printed money the proffered Argentine currency so as to maintain exchange rates in a 'dirty' float. It would then have been the case that spending in Britain had to exceed the value of goods produced. In the Argentine, spending would have just matched production since the money printed there would have been held idle, in reserve, by the Bank of England. Excess spending would cause traded goods prices to rise in the UK but this would not have prevented the Argentine from spending successfully in the UK the sterling she had acquired in exchange for her own currency. That sterling might not have bought all that was hoped for but it would have bought something. Calculated at the new prices Britain would have spent less than the value of her product. This is because the previous period's income spent in the given period would have been *less* than the value of the given period's product valued at current prices, for, if it had not been, nothing would have been left of the product for Argentinians to buy. If British spending at current prices had equaled the value of her product either the Argentine's attempts to spend her printed money, converted to sterling, would have failed, or UK prices would have risen more sharply than is assumed, which is a contradiction.

All this generates the strange situation where no one is saving and no one borrowing, yet, by courtesy of inflation, one country is consuming more than the value of its product and another country less, by exactly the same amount. Supply equals demand throughout the world yet an imbalance of trade is observed. Ex post facto, government budgets might have been balanced in both countries, yet there has been a redistribution of real expenditure between countries.

Consider now the actual clearing of markets. Figure 1 above identifies the price changes needed. In both cases treated above the Argentine price of non-traded goods would have had to rise relative to traded goods. In Britain non-traded goods would have had to fall in price relatively. The price ratio between eP_T^A, the Argentine price of traded goods, converted to sterling at an exchange rate e, and P_T^B, the sterling price of traded goods, would have had to remain unchanged in the long run.

To sketch a plausible scenario for relative price changes consistent with the argument above it is convenient to think first of the Argentine as the country with the money-printing, inflationary policy. Prices in the Argentine can be supposed to be rising while prices in Britain are not. The price P_T^A in the Argentine of traded goods will therefore have risen so that the corresponding sterling price eP_T^A is greater than P_T^B, the sterling price of traded goods in Britain. This differential would be expected to induce a switch in Argentine expenditure from traded goods produced there towards those produced in the UK. The price P_T^B would then be expected to rise relative to the price of non-traded goods as required.

Since demand for traded goods has now shifted from the Argentine to Britain the inflationary pressures originating in the Argentine must fall more heavily on non-traded goods in that country. The price P_T^A would be expected to rise more slowly than the price of non-traded goods in the Argentine. The price of non-traded goods would rise relatively as required.

To attain an equilibrium, with constant prices everywhere and cleared markets, all that is necessary is that the trade deficit generated by the Argentine should provide enough extra traded goods to absorb over each period of time all the extra money created by the Argentine in that period. If the UK countered by selling treasury bills in each period so as to raise sterling sufficient to buy the inflow of Argentinian currency there need be no inflation in Britain. But if the needed sterling were printed in each period inflation in Britain must follow. Prices P_T^B would rise in each period as the consequence of Argentinian spending of the printed sterling. The real terms of trade P_T^B/eP_T^A might be kept constant by the continuous depreciation of sterling (i.e. by a continuous upward movement in e).

From the examples and arguments given it should now be clear that there are, in the twentieth century, not only innumerably many more sets of prices that will clear markets than in the nineteenth century, each at the cost of a payments imbalance, but also innumerably many more ways in which prices might adjust. As long as world currencies continue to be issued with undefined purchasing power in any single commodity, much less commodities in general, there must be inflation. Exact control of the price level is impossible and, given the political temptations and unlimited profit opportunities afforded by 'confetti money', even partial control is close to impossible. Thus, in a world of many countries, each, with varying degrees of enthusiasm, attempting the impossible, fixed exchange rates are not to be expected.

No longer is it necessary to adjust relative prices to meet changing demands by the *reduction* of at least one price. No longer is there any need actually to *cut* a money wage. Real wages may be cut relatively by a process which allows some or all prices to rise faster than some or all wage rates. Relative prices may be adjusted the same way. This applies also between countries. International relative prices may be adjusted either by different relative rates of inflation in different countries or by exchange rate revaluation.

Inflation is not without benefits but these are short term and lead inevitably to a day of reckoning. An actual money wage cut cannot be disguised. If it is accepted as inevitable its consequence is likely to be a 'voluntary' reduction in the work force in the industry experiencing that wage cut, 'voluntary', that is, in the sense that it reflects decisions by individuals to leave, or not to join, the work force rather than a decision by the employers to declare redundancies. Price and wage cuts are an essential part of the adjustment mechanism and for that very reason *must* be sufficiently hurtful to induce action on the part of the marginal individual. If no action is induced the price mechanism has failed.

Inflation reduces economic pressures, encourages political rather than productive action and at the same time presents politicians with a cheap and effective analgesic. When the real wage cut takes the form of a money wage rise only partially offsetting continuous commodity price rises not identified directly with the necessary real wage cut, productive action is inhibited. Individuals see their personal problems as due entirely to a mysterious disease called inflation and not at all to the fact that the industry which employs them is in decline. They complain to the government which in self-defense prints more money to permit the payment of more wages. This in turn generates more inflation annihilating the effect of the wage increase. The attempt to please the electorate by printing money is a doubly cruel confidence trick. Not only does it fail to deliver the real wage increase it promises, but by the very promise, it persuades the marginal worker not to take the action that would have provided the real wage increase anyway without unnecessary meddling by the government in whom he rests his trust.

Precisely the same considerations apply in the field of international trade. Inflation and international capital movements have grossly inhibited, if not entirely suppressed, the price adjustment mechanism. We should have no expectation any longer that all real capital movements are *intended* real capital movements, everywhere recognized as such. Money capital lent by country A to country B need not have been raised by saving; nor should we expect that the transfer of money from A to B will generate pressures leading inevitably to a conscious increase in saving by individuals in A. Money transferred, if it is spent, must in one way or another induce a real reduction in consumption in A; but if this is secured by inflation no individual person in A need necessarily either be consciously aware of the cause of the reduction in consumption or be the holder of any kind of bond or IOU certifying that he is the owner of any portion of country B's debt. The debt could take the form of international currency reserves held by A's central bank, not necessarily earning interest and with no guarantee of future purchasing power. The wealth of a country can be squandered in pursuit of objectives which, if they were aware of all the implications, almost certainly would not be approved of by the proper owners of that wealth.

(vii) *The Rise and Fall of the International Monetary Fund*

The price mechanism in international trade is no different from any other price mechanism. If it is to work it must hurt. It must hurt precisely because its purpose is to induce a change in the productive behavior of individuals not otherwise aware of the need for change. Nor can the inconvenience be avoided since the inconvenience lies in the change itself and not in the signal to change. Even if there were no price system there would have to be the change.

In a world however where the primary function of government is conventionally supposed to be the protection of the individual against inconvenience it is natural for those inconvenienced to complain, just as it is natural for governments receiving complaints to seize upon any instrument that will do to satisfy supplicants, whether that satisfaction is illusory or not.

The international market mechanism actually works by facing some producers with unsold stocks and falling profits, which imply unemployment and/or reduced wages. On the other side of the coin there must be others experiencing excess demand, shortages of labor and materials and all that goes with an overheated economy. Governments, believing that they know how to 'plan' these problems away, print and distribute money, on the one hand, or save and lend, on the other. In so far as these exercises are superficially successful they simply remove the mechanism which corrects trade imbalances in a manner already adequately described, creating in the process overspending, inflation and corresponding problems in the settlement of international payments. What we actually observe are countries consistently unable to find enough internationally acceptable currency to pay their debts.

Chronic deficits seem to support the view taken by those who blame the 'lack of international liquidity'. The impossibility of making international payments, due to excess expenditure by the very countries already printing money at home, comes to be interpreted as a barrier to trade caused by lack of international money.

The International Monetary Fund was set up by planners to deal with this problem first and foremost. It was thought that if a group of countries, including the USA, could be induced to create money to be deposited in a common pool, those in deficit would be able to borrow the newly created money and so continue to trade. Of course rules were made to prevent deficit countries from becoming too much in deficit but since the Fund itself permitted deficit countries to stay in deficit the demand for even more 'liquidity' inevitably made itself felt. The history of the Fund has been the history of an organization grudgingly and under pressure seeking ways to create more and more internationally acceptable purchasing power against its better judgment. The consequence was of course that on the whole deficits persisted and grew bigger.

One inescapable consequence of permanent payment deficits has to be permanent surpluses elsewhere. And when these surpluses come to be held in the form of acceptable foreign money instead of gold reserves in the bank vaults, the temptation to onlend the funds so generated could hardly be resisted. Nor would the onlending seem unnatural to those whose business it has always been to accept deposits and find borrowers.

The importance of the IMF as a universal provider of unearned international money has declined in recent years not because of its unwillingness to do the job but because the needed funds became available elsewhere. The IMF served only to prime the pump. There can as a matter of logic be no shortage of funds. The IMF accustomed the world to the *idea* that foreign exchange might be offered at interest to the very same countries whose deficits generate the reserves they borrow. From here it is but a short step to the full scale Euro-dollar market, which is the subject of this book.

Reference

Marshall, Alfred (1923), *Money Credit and Commerce* (London: Macmillan), Book III, Ch. IX, para 1.

3 The Chronicles of the Planet Htrae

(i) *Htrae*

Professor Fred Hoyle, a distinguished cosmologist, some years ago argued that the number of stars in the universe is so great that, by the ordinary laws of chance, there must exist another planet exactly like Earth, with another cricket team indistinguishable from the MCC first eleven, playing a match on a ground similar to Lord's, against another eleven no different from that fielded by Australia.

We ourselves would not go so far as to believe this, but we do have to report that in our imagination which, as it happens, travels faster than light, we actually did locate the planet Htrae where there existed, long ago, a Namyac-Bal market not unlike the Eurodollar market here on Earth. The chronicles of the planet Htrae which we were able to study are of particular interest since they give an account, not only of the rise, but also of the fall of the Namyac-Bal. The beginnings and later growth of the Namyac-Bal market closely matched that of the Eurodollar. Whether, in due course, the end of the Eurodollar will come about in a manner even remotely resembling the collapse of the Namyac-Bal is a matter upon which we would not care to speculate, for any number of scenarios might be constructed, spectacular or unspectacular, all of which would be consistent with economic principles. Even so, there may be lessons to be learned from the contemplation of happenings the like of which have not yet been seen on Earth, particularly for those whose belief in the immutability throughout the universe of the principles governing social behavior is at all as strong as Professor Hoyle's in the logic of the theory of probability.

After the first great financial crisis on Htrae, the three countries into which the surface of the planet was partitioned came, by a sort of irresistible mass assent, to be renamed according to their pattern of economic behavior in the years immediately preceding that crisis. We have therefore, as a mnemonic, made a translation of the new names and corresponding currencies in a manner that should be at once intelligible to the Earthbound reader. All other Htrae names have been preserved and rendered as far as possible phonetically. No attempt should be made to identify the countries of Htrae with those on Earth or to seek particular parallels in behavior. Where the cap fits let it be worn, but only where it fits.

The three nations of Htrae were Surplusia, Deficitia and Balancia. In Surplusia there had been a great inflation. Following this experience the government of Surplusia determined on an austere policy calling for a budget surplus and the repayment of past debt. Deficitia, on the other hand, had elected a socialist government which believed in public spending and the large scale printing of money. Deficitia's total expenditure (including expenditure on capital creation) always exceeded the value of its production, while Surplusia bought (including capital) goods of less value than it produced. Balancia pursued the middle way. The government of Balancia regularly spent only what it raised in taxation, the printing of money being prohibited. Balancia was renowned for its stable currency and its banking community for its probity and reliability. Money invested in Balancia was everywhere considered to be in safe hands.

Throughout the planet Htrae all markets were cleared. International trade flourished and supply everywhere was just sufficient to meet demand. Deficit spending in Deficitia exactly matched underspending in Surplusia. The excess of goods produced by Surplusia over and above its consumption needs were exported to the rest of the planet. Deficitia succeeded in consuming more than it produced by importing more from the rest of the planet than it exported. Balancia's imports were of course just paid for by its exports. Surplusia enjoyed an excess of exports over imports and a currency inflow from Deficitia equal in value to Deficitia's overspending.

At first Surplusia was content to receive and hold units of Deficitia's currency (the Def) in the form of foreign currency reserves. In practice the Surplusian banks held Def deposits in banks in Deficitia. Surplusia, in short, exchanged goods for Defs. Year by year Surplusia's Def balances at banks in Deficitia grew larger and larger. Nevertheless no inflation could be observed in any one of the three countries of Htrae for the following reason.

In Deficitia the government financed its budget deficit by requiring the banking system to buy Treasury Bills in such a way that the ratio of central bank deposits to total deposits remained constant. Total deposits grew each year by an amount equal to the growth of Surplusian deposits in Deficitian banks. Open market operations by the Deficitian central bank maintained the traditional cash ratio. No additional money was ever created to finance deficit spending by the private sector, for there was none. The new money introduced each year was never more than that needed to buy Surplusia's overproduction so that prices remained constant. At the end of each year the addition to the money stock could be seen in the accounts of the banking sector as a growth in the balances which formed the (idle) Surplusian currency reserve.

By contrast the Surplusian budget surplus was used by government to buy back Surplusian government bonds from a stock held by its own banking system, accumulated during the inflation era. The Surps so passing to the banking system were bought by Deficitian importers in exchange for Def deposits. Importers naturally used the Surps thus acquired to pay for excess exports from Surplusia, thereby returning them to the country of origin. The amount of money circulating in Surplusia remained constant as did its level of production. The inflation rate was zero. Supply found itself equal to demand in all markets.

(ii) *The Beginnings of the Namyac-Bal Market*

Despite the happy condition of equilibrium in all markets, bankers in Deficitia were not content. They understood the need to maintain the traditional cash/deposit ratio but they understood also that the more money they could lend the greater would be their profit. Furthermore they had observed that the ratio of checks drawn per month to total deposits and hence to cash was diminishing year by year, not because activity was diminishing but because idle balances owned by Surplusia were growing. Foreign deposits formed a larger and larger proportion of total deposits but no checks were ever drawn on them. There seemed less and less likelihood of banks not being able to meet their cash needs precisely at a time when the ratio of bank profits to total cash was diminishing.

At this point the germ of an idea developed in the mind of one of the directors of Erehwon bank in Deficitia. Off the coast of the country there existed a small group of atolls known collectively as the Namyac islands which were uninhabited and, since they boasted no natural resources, were claimed by no one. Why not found the Republic of Namyac and set up a bank? Such a bank would be subject only to the laws of the new republic and would not be limited by a cash ratio. Of course, it would not enjoy the advantage of being able to turn to a lender of last resort either but this was not the problem as the bankers saw it.

Erehwon Bank (International) was duly founded and commenced operations at once. Surplusian holders of Def deposits in Deficitia were encouraged, by offers of higher interest rates, to switch their deposits to Erehwon (International) in the Namyac Republic. Funds so deposited were then onlent to Erehwon (Head Office) in Deficitia, so that government Treasury Bills could be bought with the Surplusian reserve as before. Now, however, the accounts of Erehwon (Head Office) looked different. Instead of Surplusian deposits among their liabilities there appeared only the counterpart deposits (loans) of the International branch; and under Deficitian banking laws no cash reserve was called for against liabilities to subsidiary banks. Erehwon (Head Office) obviously held more cash than was needed to meet its statutory obligation as well as more cash than it felt necessary to cover its expected transactions turnover. Besides taking up its customary quota of Treasury Bills it was able to make loans to the private sector of the order of ten times its excess of cash. Income from this source made it possible to pay a higher interest rate than normal on the Erehwon (International) deposits, at the same time leaving a handsome profit for Erehwon (Head Office).

Of course the central bank in Deficitia might well have countered the Erehwon bank innovation by refusing to buy its share (one tenth) of the Treasury Bill issue needed to finance the government deficit; but it was already too late for this. The new money for the current year had already been created and lent. There was now an excess demand for goods in both Deficitia and, because of higher Deficitian imports, in Surplusia. Prices rose in both countries. Deficitia devalued its currency and the central bank ceased to purchase Treasury Bills leaving the whole issue to commercial banks. Surplusia, still remembering its earlier inflation experience, added to its budget surplus as a deflationary measure. Price and market equilibrium, but not trade balance, were restored.

Because of the Deficitian inflation, Surplusia now became worried about the risk attached to its holding of Defs. Already Surplusian banks had suffered a capital loss as a consequence of Deficitia's devaluation. The Surplusian government insisted that henceforth all payments for Surplusian exports should be made in Balancia's currency, the Bal, for this was known to be the planet's safest money.

Fortunately for Deficitia, one of its banks held a very modest reserve of 1 million Bals on deposit in a Balancian bank. A Deficitian trader who imported oil from Surplusia was the first to apply for Balancian currency to pay the exporter in Surplusia. In exchange for a check in Defs drawn on the oil importer's bank the Deficitian bank with the Bal deposit gave the importer a check for 1 million Bals drawn against the bank in Balancia where its Bals were deposited. The oil having been paid for, the Bal deposit in Balancia passed in due course into the possession of the bank in Surplusia which negotiated the exporter's check in exchange for Surps. What should a bank do with unwanted Bals? Put them out, of course, where they will earn the highest interest, that is, deposit them with Erehwon (International) — Namyac. Erehwon (International) stood ready to receive time deposits and make loans designated in any of the planet's currencies.

In the meantime a second importer of oil in Deficitia applied to his bank for Bals but the bank had none. Never mind, Erehwon (International) now owned Bals, lent by Surplusia out of oil proceeds, all ready to lend to the Deficitian bank at, naturally, a slightly higher rate of interest than that paid to Surplusia. The very same 1 million Bal deposit, originally a Deficitian deposit in a Balancian bank, now a Deficitian deposit borrowed from Erehwon (International), sets off once again around the circuit arriving eventually back in a borrowing bank in Deficitia all ready to buy a new consignment of oil all over again, and so on.

In truth nothing had really changed. Surplusia found itself lending the proceeds of its excess of exports to Deficitia just as before. The only difference was that Surplusia did not know this. Its bankers believed that they were lending on a short-term basis and in a safe currency (Bals) to Erehwon (International), presumably a safe bank. They hardly realized that Erehwon (International) was in fact onlending their Bal savings to Deficitia in a manner no different from the earlier *direct* loans by Surplusia to Deficitia, executed by leaving Def deposits untouched in Deficitian banks. The fact that under the new system the loans were designated in Bals instead of Defs made no difference to the real situation. The effect was psychological only. Surplusians felt more comfortable holding Bal deposits than they did Def deposits so they continued to hold rather than spend their balances.

As before, Deficitian banks were supplied with funds to

finance their government's annual budget deficit. Importers of oil in Deficitia had to pay Defs for the Bal currency needed to pay Surplusia. Against their borrowings of Bals in the Namyac-Bal market, therefore, Deficitian banks found themselves holding Defs. These funds they lent to government to earn the going return on government bonds. Of course, Deficitian banks did then have to tolerate liabilities designated in Bals covered only by assets designated in Defs; but they secured their position quite simply by entering into suitable forward contracts to buy Bals on the dates that their Bal debts were due. In the event, Surplusian holders of Bal deposits in the Namyac-Bal market rolled over their deposits on the due date as did Erehwon (International) its loans to Erehwon (Head Office).

Surprisingly, Deficitian forward contracts in the foreign exchange market had no long-term effect upon the exchange rate between Defs and Bals. The reason was quite simple. At the slightest hint of a rise in the forward price of Bals expressed in Defs, Balancia's central bank entered equal and opposite contracts to buy Defs so as to protect their forward exchange rate.

(iii)   *The Stock of Money in Deficitia*

Notice especially that although Deficitia's debt to the Namyac-Bal market (henceforth called the N.B. market) grew continuously by the amount of the annual budget deficit, nevertheless the money stock measured by total deposits and cash did not grow at all.

The temporary phenomenon which led Deficitia's banks to establish the N.B. market in the first place had by this time disappeared. Erehwon (Head Office) debt to Erehwon (International) did not count as deposits. The central bank, as explained above, ceased buying government bonds entirely. The credit base remained constant as did the total Def money supply. Government needs were met entirely by the sales of new securities to the banks in exchange for Defs surrendered on the purchase of Erehwon (International) Bals. Defs so surrendered were returned into circulation in Deficitia as a result of government deficit spending. The trade imbalance continued as before. Planet 'equilibrium' persisted. Once again no inflation was observed in any country.

(iv)   *The Astonishing Expansion of the N.B. Market*

Despite the constancy of each individual producing country's stock of money, deposits in the N.B. market continued to grow at a rapid rate. Indeed, since Deficitia was the largest country on Htrae, and since it had introduced a 'social wage' so generous that it could not possibly find the money to finance it out of taxation by a sum in Defs equal to 10 percent of Deficitia's gross national product (which in turn was five times larger than that of Balancia), deposits in the N.B. market amounted each year to the equivalent of one half of the gross national product of Balancia. The size, measured in deposits, of the N.B. market in a very few years came to Bals 1,000,000,000,000, that is, three times the total of all the money in Balancia. Some commentators argued that there must be double counting. They eliminated all debt owed by or to banks, thereby proving conclusively that there was no N.B. market there at all. Other commentators argued that a 'multiplier' was at work, claiming that the N.B. market must be lending Bals that it had not got, just as an ordinary commercial bank lends money it has not got when it furnishes Mr A. N. Rehto with a check book and a deposit account, allowing him to pay bills against a 'loan' of the amount shown on deposit. Those who argued this way were clearly wrong since at no time did Erehwon (International) issue a checkbook to anyone. Surplusian Bal deposits were all 'time' deposits which could not be withdrawn or even transferred to another owner. Such time deposits could not be used by Surplusia to finance further transactions, nor were the Surplusians in need of finance. It was precisely because they were in trade surplus that deposits were made in Erehwon (International) in the first place. Erehwon time deposits were not money and could not be used as money. Only on the due date was Erehwon (International) obligated to draw a check on its Bal deposits in Deficitia so as to be able to repay its Surplusian creditor. And in each case, when the due date arrived Surplusia had agreed to 'roll-over' the funds, that is, to redeposit for a further time period. Erehwon (International) was never required to repay nor could its bank, Erehwon (Head Office), ever have met the Bal check even if drawn. Deficitia owned no Bals, only Defs. To secure Bals it would have been necessary for Erehwon (Head Office) to exercise its forward option in the foreign exchange market to buy Bals.

As a matter of fact Erehwon (International) did not even have a checkbook that would permit it to draw a check on its Bal deposits in head office. In order to be in a position to pay interest on Surplusian time deposits with itself, Erehwon (International) was bound to onlend these deposits to Erehwon (Head Office) equally on a time deposit basis. Only time deposits yield interest and Erehwon (International) enjoyed no other net income than the difference between the high interest rates paid to it by Erehwon (Head Office) and the slightly lower rates it paid to the Surplusian depositors of the funds onlent.

To defend itself against the charge of imprudent banking, Erehwon (International) claimed that it was not really a bank. Its function it suggested was simply that of a financial intermediary — an accepting house which did no more than underwrite the debt of Deficitia to Surplusia. Surplusia did not trust either Deficitian banks or Deficitian currency, the Def. It did, however, trust the Bal and believed, quite wrongly, that so long as it held Bals, Balancia was the country with the ultimate responsibility for the repayment of its deposits, simply because they were designated in Bals. Never was a confidence trick more neatly executed!

Erehwon (International) equally protested that no risk of default existed even though no reserves of 'real money' were held against the Surplusian deposits. It claimed to have 'matched' the maturities of its deposits and loans. For every deposit falling due for repayment Erehwon (International) claimed that it had a loan of equal magnitude falling due on the same day. On the other hand, enquiries proved that the N.B. market (Erehwon International) was not being entirely truthful in this matter. Like all financial intermediaries (e.g. building societies) Erehwon (International) tended to borrow short and lend long. It believed, however, that if the worst came to the worst it could always sell some of its long-dated assets at very short notice at a modest loss; or, in circumstances worse than the worst, seek support from Erehwon (Head Office) and/or the Deficitian central bank.

(v)   *Was the N.B. Market Inflationary?*

Many economists on Htrae before the rise of the N.B. market believed that all bank deposits, whether sight or time, should be counted in the money stock. Unanimously they argued that all financial assets are money in some degree. All can in some sense be spent. Few really appreciated the full implications of the simple fact of life that all that can ever be spent is that which is acceptable in payment. In other words, before it can be spent a time deposit must be exchanged for a check drawn on some bank, that is, an instrument that will serve to secure an increase in the payee's current account deposits. In order to spend a financial asset, it is necessary first to sell it to someone who holds money. In the case of N.B. market deposits, there did not exist enough true money in the whole planet to effect repayment, much less to ensure that a buyer could be found for all sellers of N.B. debt.

The belief that N.B. market deposits really were money became a source of embarrassment to Htrae economists precisely because it was a mistaken belief. Theory and fact were in obvious contradiction. It proved impossible to agree simultaneously to the inclusion of N.B. market deposits in the definition of the money stock *and* to the validity of the obvious rule that

$$MV = PT$$

that is, that the money stock, M, times the velocity of circulation, V, must be identical to the product of prices, P, and the number of transactions, T.

Indeed, on the definitions favored, the money stock in Htrae had risen in a few years by Bals 1,000,000,000,000 during which period neither prices nor the volume of transactions per period of time had changed one jot, apart that is from the relatively very small temporary initial movement that induced the establishment of the N.B. market in the first place. World transactions rates remained constant. The N.B. market could not have been inflationary since no inflation was observed.

Nor on reflection could the economists on Htrae identify anything that might comfortably be called a reduction in the velocity of circulation of money. It came to be understood that N.B. market deposits were not of themselves money. Their presence simply recorded the fact that money had changed hands between borrowers and lenders. The true money had long since been spent and could not be conjured back into the hands of depositors until some other person or institution currently holding money could be induced to buy the debt owned by Erehwon (International). Evidently the existence of the N.B. deposits was not of itself inflationary.

(vi)   *The Role of Balancia in the N.B. Market*

Before their study of the N.B. market Htrae economists had always supposed that only central banks could create money. If more and more Bals seemed to appear on the planet, the fault must lie with the Federal Reserve Bank of Balancia. But once again Htrae economists were embarrassed by the facts. In what way could the Balancian bank authorities be held to be responsible for the fourfold multiplication of Bal deposits on the planet when

(1)   The Balancian home money stock remained constant.
(2)   Balancia lent no money to anyone.

(3) Balancia consistently generated neither surplus nor deficit in international trade.

(4) Although Balancia constantly entered into forward contracts to sell Bals, at no time did it actually sell more than was necessary to pay for its imports.

(5) No other active policy fiscal or monetary was pursued by Balancia. No positive act that would account for the phenomenon under review could be identified.

Htrae economists finally conceded that the existence and growth of the N.B. market could not in any way be attributed to Balancia even though transactions in that market were conducted almost exclusively in Bals.

(vii) *Controlling National Money Supplies*

Simple developments in economic institutions never stay simple for long. And so it was with the N.B. market on Htrae. The lead given by Erehwon (International) was soon followed by other banks with head offices located elsewhere than in Deficitia. Branch banks in the Republic of Namyac seeking borrowers for Bals deposited by Surplusia found other clients not confined to the relatively small group of Deficitian banks selling Bals for Defs to Deficitian importers. They made loans designated in Bals direct to Deficitian industrialists for investment in plant and buildings. Bals so introduced into the Deficitian economy were exchanged for Defs by the central bank and passed into the national currency reserve.

Economists in Deficitia in consequence of the new development became alarmed by the apparent impossibility of controlling the money supply. What, they argued, is the use of the central bank engaging in open market operations to restrict the supply of Defs, so as to control potential inflation in Deficitia, when anyone who wished might quite easily obtain apparently unrestricted sums of money from the N.B. market to spend in Deficitia. Royal Commissions were set up to enquire into the need for control over the operations of the

N.B. market. Suggestions were made that N.B. operators should be required to hold cash reserves and be subject to banking regulations.

More thoughtful economists, however, were puzzled by the undeniable fact that no inflation at all could be observed in any country despite the seemingly large inflow of Bals. After much study of the problem they came to understand that debt is not money unless the debt instrument can be passed from hand to hand in settlement of other debt. As long as real money is not created for the purpose no amount of borrowing and lending can ever cause inflation.

Bals lent from overseas to Deficitian investors were not newly created; they were saved by the Surplusian government where taxes and/or loans from the private sector exceeded government expenditure. The Bals so saved passed via the N.B. market to individuals in Deficitia and/or to the Deficitian government so that national expenditure in Deficitia might (and did) exceed income (i.e. the Deficitian GNP) by precisely the amount saved. The trade imbalance between Deficitia and Surplusia existed *because of* the spending and saving habits of the two countries. No inflation or unemployment existed in either country for the very reason that Surplusia provided the goods which Deficitia over-consumed and was content to hold debt in exchange. The debt, however, was debt and not money. As before, Surplusians *thought* they were lending safe money in a safe N.B. market bank and would not, perhaps, have been willing to hold direct debt.

Of course, inflation *would* have occurred if anywhere along the chain money *had* been created. But in the first instance it was not.

(viii) *The First Great Crisis on Htrae*

Unfortunately, it was not long before the very existence of the N.B. market itself induced some central banks to create real money where no corresponding goods to buy existed. The sequence of events was initiated primarily by the widespread belief that Bal-designated debt in the N.B. market, now amounting to several times the entire annual gross national product of Balancia, was somehow a liability of Balancia, just because it was expressed in Bals. This coupled with a political scandal in Balancian high places was sufficient to induce a loss of confidence in the Bal in banking circles in Surplusia. As Surplusian loans to the N.B. market fell due for repayment, banks in Surplusia refused to make any roll-over arrangement. Instead they demanded repayment, with the intention of relending in Surps. This forced the N.B. market, now much extended by operations of a great many imitators of Erehwon (International), to refuse in their turn to renew Bal loans to Deficitia. But Deficitian banks owned no Bals with which to make repayment of their debt. Their assets consisted only of Def-designated advances and Treasury Bills. They proceeded therefore to sell Treasury Bills for Defs and sought to exercise their options (previously bought on the forward market) to buy Bals in the foreign exchange markets. Exchange rates moved in favor of Bals and against Defs. Balancia, anxious to protect its exporters against currency appreciation, entered into a 'swap' arrangement with Deficitia. The Balancian central bank agreed to open a deposit account, designated in Bals in favor of the Deficitian bank, the quid pro quo being an equivalent deposit account, designated in Defs, opened by the Deficitian central bank in favor of the Balancian central bank. Each bank gained an asset and a liability of equal value but each was now able to draw checks on the other, designated in the other's currency. Both banks had *created money*. Where did this money go? We trace it as follows.

Deficitian commercial banks could now buy Bals from their own central bank in exchange for Defs raised by the sale of Treasury Bills to the public. But the sale of Treasury Bills raised the rate of interest so that the central bank was induced to buy bills in an 'open market operation'. In effect, therefore, commercial banks simply exchanged Treasury Bills for Bals at the central bank, paying the Bals to the N.B. banks in discharge of their debt. The Bals newly created by the swap agreement accordingly passed into the hands of the N.B. banks who promptly paid their depositors in Surplusia. But Surplusian depositors had demanded their Bals only because of their mistrust of this currency. Their intent was to exchange them for Surps as soon as possible. Accordingly they instructed their banks in Surplusia to sell Bals for Surps, an exercise which depressed the Bal exchange rate. Balancia was thus impelled once again to make a swap agreement, this time with Surplusia. The Surplusian central bank raised a Surp-designated deposit in favor of the Balancian central bank in exchange for Bal deposits raised in the Balancian central bank in favor of the Surplusian central bank. Armed with a supply of newly created Surps the bank then entered the exchange market to buy Bals for Surps, thereby restoring the exchange rate to normal.

Four separate tranches of money had up to this point been created by swap agreements, one of Defs, two of Bals, and one of Surps. The Defs remained in the hands of the Balancian central bank (deposits in the Deficitian central bank). The first tranche of Bals had annihilated itself as follows. It came into being with the swap agreement between Balancia and Deficitia, taking the form of a Deficitian deposit with the Balancian central bank. Checks had been drawn on this account, which were endorsed over to the N.B. market banks in settlement of Deficitian debt, endorsed again by the N.B. market banks with an order to pay their Surplusian creditors and finally endorsed again in favor of the Balancian central bank as it sold its newly acquired Surps for the very same Bals it had created for Deficitia under the original swap agreement. Deficitian deposits in Balancia were accordingly reduced once more to zero.

The second tranche of Bals arising from the second swap agreement (Surplusian central bank Bal deposits in the Balancian central bank) remained where they were.

The Balancian central bank Surp deposits created by the second swap agreement were now of course in the hands of Surplusian citizens who had formerly held deposits in Bals in N.B. market banks. Since the holders of the Surps did not wish to consume goods but only to buy a safer financial asset they invested in Surplusian Treasury Bills, thereby depressing interest rates. The Surplusian central bank accordingly sold bills to restore the interest rate level, thereby annihilating a sum in Surps equal to that created by the swap agreement.

Only two tranches of newly created money therefore survived, Surplusia's Bal deposits in Balancia and Balancia's Def deposits in Deficitia, both of which now formed part of these countries' exchange reserves held by their central banks.

At this point all would have been well were it not for the fact that central banks are frequently managed by talented 'bankers' rather than by 'central bankers'. It was observed that higher rates of interest were offered for deposits in N.B. banks than in central banks whatever the currency designation. The Surplusian central bank deposited its excess Bals and the Balancian central bank its excess Defs in the N.B. market in Namyac. To pay the higher rates of interest to their depositors N.B. market banks sought to lend to less and less respectable borrowers at even higher rates of interest. Respectable banks onlent to less respectable banks which onlent to positively unrespectable borrowers.

Worst of all, the money now being injected into various countries was money that had been created by swap agreements. It permitted every country to spend more than its citizens earned by production *without any other country necessarily spending less than it earned*. Planet-wide ex-ante demand exceeded planet-wide ex-ante supply. Planet-wide inflation followed.

Of course, in an ex-post sense, apart from stock changes, not every country could *succeed* in consuming more than it produced. Those countries that borrowed the greater part of the 'printed' money consumed most and suffered balance of payments deficits. Those who borrowed least enjoyed surpluses which were redeposited in the N.B. market in ever increasing quantities. *The facilities afforded by the N.B. market destroyed the very mechanism that would have served to adjust the balance of payments and would paradoxically have removed the need for the N.B. market.*

Exchange rates, rates of interest and balance of payments were subjected to wild and unpredictable fluctuations, provoking greater and greater uncertainty and, of course, more and more desperate attempts to switch accumulated international debt from one currency denomination to another. More swap agreements were generated and more unwanted money pumped into the system.

Exchange rates came to be determined entirely by frantic operations in the now staggeringly large market for debt and not at all by the establishment of purchasing power parity in traded goods. The whole pattern of trade itself became destabilized. Production was affected and unemployment grew. Each of the three countries with characteristic inconsistency tried both to control its money supply and to use the rate of interest as a means of attracting foreign currency to balance international payments.

(ix)   *Aftermath*

At the height of the chaos a small group of economists and bankers, wise enough to be aware that they did not wholly understand those things that it was their business to understand, sought to rethink the whole process from the beginning.

First they asked what might have happened if central banks in Surplusia and Balancia had not redeposited their Bal and Def balances in the N.B. market but instead had held them idle in the form of deposits in Balancia and Deficitia, respectively. They observed that there would not then have been any planet-wide inflation arising out of the swap agreements.

Next they asked themselves what might have happened if citizens in Surplusia, having successfully exchanged their Bal deposits in the N.B. market for Surps, had chosen themselves to redeposit their Surps directly in the N.B. market rather than to buy Surplusian Treasury Bills. Deficitia might then have borrowed these Surps so as to be able to engage in a three-cornered 'negative' swap agreement as follows. With a suitable endorsement of checks the Deficitian central bank might have offered its borrowed Surps to the Balancian central bank in exchange for a check for an equivalent amount of Defs drawn on the Balancian Def account in the Deficitian central bank. This would have annihilated the Defs created in the first swap agreement. Balancia would have had the Surps which might then have been endorsed over to Surplusia in exchange for a Bal check drawn on Surplusia's central bank Bal account in the Balancian central bank. This would have annihilated simultaneously both the Bals and the Surps created by the second swap agreement between Balancia and Surplusia. The net effect of all these transactions and those that went before would simply have been to redesignate some part of the Deficitian Bal debt to the N.B. market as an equivalent sum in Surps, and to redesignate the corresponding Bal debt of the N.B. market to Surplusia also into Surps. The whole exercise achieved nothing except to satisfy Surplusian creditors as to the safety of their investments. The new money created by the swap agreements was simply money needed to effect the transactions. As soon as the transactions were concluded the money needed for the purpose should have been annihilated. The fact that some part of it was not annihilated but rather onlent to the N.B. market was one of the major causes of the inflation. Purchasing power was made available which had been generated by banking activities rather than by production.

These reflections led the Commission of Enquiry to perceive that the N.B. market might just as well have met the wishes of its Surplusian creditors by asking for a roll-over agreement which included a redesignation of the currency unit as well as a renegotiation of the term. The Bal debt could have been rolled over in Surps. And to cover themselves the N.B. banks might equally have insisted that Deficitia's Bal debt to themselves should be rolled over in Surps. No money need have been created at all. Swap agreements which caused the problem are quite unnecessary. Inflation is generated not only by the mistaken belief that all economic problems can be solved by spending printed money. It is generated also by banks seeking to protect other banks from the consequences of their own misbehavior.

At the same time it was brought home even more forcefully to the commission that debt is debt and not money and that money is money and not debt. Debt is the liability of the debtor and not of the country in whose currency unit the debt is designated. Money is created by banks. Debt can be finally annihilated only by goods. But debt can be exchanged for goods *only* if it is first exchanged for money. Banks are under no legal obligation to give goods for money. They are required only to transfer money from one person to another on demand. Only if the owner of money, legitimately acquired by the production of goods *currently on offer for sale*, is prepared to exchange money for debt is it possible to exchange debt for goods without inflation.

Above all the commission came to see even more clearly that although debt may be passed from person to person it ordinarily requires money to transfer it. Buying and selling debt is no different from buying and selling goods. Money is needed to sustain the transactions.

(x)   *The End of the First Crisis*

The commission was fortunate in getting a hearing for its findings despite the myriad of voices offering contradictory advice. Central bank swap agreements were banned. Money was more carefully distinguished from debt and closer control exercised. It was everywhere agreed that international debt could be rolled over in any currency according to the wishes of the creditor. Inflation abated and public confidence was restored. Unfortunately that very confidence planted the seed of a new disaster.

(xi) *The Final Collapse*

During the early days of the N.B. market, banks had taken care to match the dates of maturity of their loans with those of their deposits. They were acutely aware they owed allegiance to no one and did not enjoy the advantage of an 'official' lender of last resort. At the same time, however, they were vaguely aware that their activities could not be described as 'traditional banking'. Banks are supposed to borrow short and lend long. Their incomes derive from the difference between short and long rates.

Officially, N.B. market banks could look for no such differential. As they could not appeal to any lender of last resort, they could lay claim to prudence only if their lending periods matched their borrowings exactly. This meant of course that they were bound to rely for their income on their 'good name'. As with any old-fashioned accepting house each bank had to appear a safer borrower than the clients to whom it lent the borrowed funds.

At a later stage the N.B. banks ceased to maintain the practice they preached. They borrowed short and lent long, defending themselves by saying that, if pressed, they could always raise money. The N.B. market they argued was by now so 'efficient' that member banks would in every case be able to exchange maturities so as to meet any individual bank's temporary needs. Little by little the overall position of the market moved towards short deposits and long loans.

Gradually the more astute members of the N.B. banking fraternity became worried. Total international indebtedness continued to grow at an annual rate of 25 percent. Rescue operations had to be instituted for one or two smaller banks. Interbank debt grew more and more complex with central banks heavily involved. Some N.B. banks like Erehwon (International) had head offices of commercial bank status with rights to appeal to the central banks of their country of origin as lender of last resort. Some were entirely independent of any of the three main countries of Htrae.

Worried N.B. bankers sought to establish agreements by central banks or bank consortia to underwrite all operations, and in some measure they were successful. At this point, however, the total international debt accrued was larger than the sum of all the money on the planet.

The end came with a revolution in Surplusia. Leaders of the revolution were inward looking 'idealists' who disapproved of 'capitalism'. They demanded the repayment in Surps of all outstanding debt due to them, believing that debt to be money lent to regimes of which they did not approve. N.B. banks, of course, could not oblige, nor were they legally required to. As Surplusia's deposits fell due for repayment, however, Surplusia refused to roll over the debt. N.B. banks therefore refused to roll over Deficitia's debt to them, now almost entirely designated in Surps. Not enough Surps were forthcoming, partly because N.B. banks had lent long but also because Deficitian banks had long since given up the practice of buying Surps forward to cover their maturities. Their confidence in the N.B. market itself had made this practice seem unnecessary. The price of Surps on the exchanges rose rather than fell despite what had earlier been regarded as a 'dangerous overhang' of Surp deposits in the N.B. market.

All the central bank and consortia underwriting agreements were invoked but no one could find Surps for the simple reason that nobody outside of Surplusia owned any. The supply of Surps arising from Deficitian and Balancian exports to Surplusia was avidly competed for, both by importers and by banks seeking to repay Surplusian creditors or to support associated banks with Surplusian creditors. Furthermore, the greater the insistence by Surplusia on the repayment of its debt the greater grew the shortage of Surps and the greater was the appreciation of the Surp relative to other currencies. On the other hand, despite the increasing profitability of exports to Surplusia there was no great rise in the total earnings of Surps from exports; for there was little scope for increased production of exportables and no decline, on the scale called for, in home demand, despite sharp price rises measured in Bals and Defs.

Many N.B. banks were forced to declare themselves unable to pay and to go into liquidation. Central banks were unable to help since swap agreements were prohibited. In any case the sums of money involved were so huge that no central bank could conceive of creating money on such a scale.

Alarmed by the rapid disappearance of what the monetary experts had previously supposed to be safe currencies deposited in reliable banks, Surplusia now demanded repayment in gold. Many banks tried to comply, seeking to buy gold with Bals or Defs. Central banks, in an attempt to support this move, created huge sums of money by raising deposits in favor of N.B. banks (head offices and subsidiaries). Balancia, of course, was equally affected since she also had established banks operating in the N.B. market. The money so created generated huge profits for the holders of gold who in consequence sought to buy consumer goods with their gains. Planet-wide inflation reached unparalleled heights.

More and more N.B. banks collapsed as the gold experiment failed. Surplusia then refused point blank to pay in Surps for its imports from Deficitia and Balancia, so an embargo was placed on further exports by both countries. Production in export industries collapsed. No acceptable form of payment to Surplusia could be found for Surplusian exports to the rest of the planet. Surplusia therefore refused to export.

Unfortunately, Surplusia had exported mainly essential and irreplaceable means of production, mostly oil. Without an energy source, production in Deficitia and Balancia collapsed and with it the entire structure of the N.B. market. Gross national products in all countries fell to less than one quarter of what they had been.

The commission of wise men, whose recommendations had rescued the planet on the occasion of the first crisis, was reconvened.

(xii) *Diagnosis*

It did not take the commission long to realize that the planet-wide collapse had come about not because the N.B. market existed but because it had grown so big that the stock of debt overwhelmed the flow of trade which had created the stock. Why had the stock so grown?

Clearly the sum total of international debt must grow as long as the same countries remain in surplus and deficit all the time. The *only* way to reduce the size of the N.B. market would have been to require Deficitia to spend less than the value of its product and Surplusia to spend more. Deficitia would then have the export surplus and Surplusia the deficit. Instead of lending money to Surplusia, Deficitia would be able to pay off its debt to the N.B. market which, ipso facto, would have no alternative but to pay off its debt to Surplusia. Surplusia would then have all the money needed to finance its high level of imports.

Not only would this have reduced the total of international debt, it would at the same time have diminished the number of banks operating, as well as their profitability. Many banks can live on the proceeds of one-eighth of 1 percent per annum of one thousand billion Bals, but not even one bank can live on the proceeds of as much as 100 percent of nothing at all. Financial intermediaries live upon imbalances.

The commission now turned its attention to the problem of *why* Surplusia was always in surplus and Deficitia always in deficit. At once they saw that it was the N.B. market itself which made this possible. *The evil of the N.B. market was that it destroyed the very mechanism which, ordinarily, forces every country to balance its international payments, that is, to live within its means.*

If a country's accumulation of debt is visible to all and if its borrowing is clearly used to finance consumption rather than investment and if the interest on the debt is obviously being paid simply by borrowing still more, then the lender will cease to lend. It will no longer be possible to consume more than is produced and the trade imbalance generated by borrowing must disappear.

If, on the other hand, the borrowing is disguised by the presence of many financial intermediaries, who are outwardly respectable and at the same time believe themselves to be protected from their own propensity to overextend by supposed lenders of last resort, then the borrowing and lending might well go on to the point where such a huge debt is accumulated that no lender of last resort could ever help.

If, at the same time, interbank lending becomes so complex that enormous sums of money can be created by central banks in such a way that no one ever notices the event, then inflation can, by still further masking, exacerbate the problem beyond all imagining. Inflation wipes out debt. It is not necessary for a borrower ever to worry about an interest rate on his debt of 15 percent per annum if the rate of inflation is 20 percent. Banks can live and thrive on a negative real rate of interest provided only that the nominal rate is greater than zero. The improvident may go on borrowing for ever if their borrowing is disguised by a financial intermediary to give respectability and if the rate of inflation is greater than or equal to the nominal rate of interest.

The commission wondered at length about the kind of institutions they might recommend to ensure that the crisis they were enduring should never occur again. A careful study of the literature revealed, to their surprise and consternation, that all of the principles, of which the events on Htrae were simply a realization, had long since been understood and written about. Nothing, they came to understand, was new. In its different contexts all that they had seen had happened before.

Many books were found detailing, in their different ways, the working of the system, pointing out, at the same time, the dangers of tampering with it. There were indeed quite ancient writings containing specific proposals designed to prevent, if not the observed occurrences, at least the nearest thing to those occurrences which could have been imagined at the time of writing. The commission quickly realized that at least one set of proposals, discussed in a book by Professor Rovi Ecraep entitled *Lanoitanretni Edart* (Pearce, 1970), if they had been implemented at the time, would have been sufficient to rule out any possibility of a Namyac-Bal market and hence any possibility of the very problems they were now summoned to confront.

Rovi Ecraep and his colleague Nerraw Nagoh were summoned to appear before them. 'Why,' they were asked, 'is it possible, when so much is already known, that disasters of the magnitude we have just witnessed seem not to be avoidable?'

Professor Ecraep replied, 'There are those whose aim is to understand and there are those who seek to influence events. To succeed even partially in either of these endeavors demands a lifetime of effort. No man therefore is able to do both.'

Reference

Pearce, I. F. (1970), *International Trade* (London: Macmillan), pp. 100–10.

4 Eurofinancing in Practice

(i) *The Beginnings*

Large scale arrangements which permit banks and other financial intermediaries to draw upon and lend funds in currencies other than that of the country in which the lender is domiciled are of quite recent development. The system is however no more than a natural extension of previously well-established practices whereby European banks, especially those based in London, used externally held US dollars for the financing of companies engaged in foreign trade. Financial institutions, broadly defined as banks, borrowed funds held as balances in New York and lent in that currency rather than the national currency of the economy in which they were located. Thus, by the late 1950s, it had become quite usual for financial intermediaries to offer deposit and lending facilities denominated in arbitrarily specified currencies rather than to deal at all times in the national currency, with foreign exchange transactions directly controlled on each occasion by national monetary authorities.

The impetus given to these developments by acts directed to quite different ends can be perceived as an apt commentary on the ironies of history. Exchange controls and monetary restraints applied by the British government restricted sterling funds available for the financing of trade between countries other than the UK. Efforts to maintain London as an international center encouraged a search for sources of funds outside of the UK, which led to the taking of deposits in dollars for this purpose. Later dollar deposits were used to finance exports and imports of the UK itself. These external dollar accounts were the embryonic form of the markets now familiar for the taking of deposits and the making of loans in foreign currencies. At the same time authorities in the Soviet Union and other centrally planned economies, recognizing the sovereign risk of holding dollar balances in New York during periods of international tension, tended to transfer all but minimum balances to their own commercial banks in London and Paris, for example, the Moscow Narodny Bank, or banks other than American ones in those centers. At a later stage, efforts by the USA to control its balance of payments induced borrowers to seek foreign held dollars to satisfy their needs. The Interest Equalization Tax, implemented by the USA in 1964, discouraged the issuing of foreign bonds on the local market; this stimulated Eurofinancing in dollar bonds through London. Complementary measures to restrain the granting of bank loans to foreign corporations and to hold down the level of foreign investment by American companies financed from within the USA still further encouraged the expansion of 'offshore' borrowings in dollars. The supply of 'foreign' dollars was yet again augmented in the late 1960s by the US authorities imposing interest ceilings on deposit rates, so pushing banks and companies to seek higher returns in foreign markets.

All of the foregoing refers, of course, only to the accumulation and use as a means of debt settlement, by and between non-US citizens, of 'true' US dollars, that is, of dollar deposits in checking accounts or their equivalent in banks located in the USA. It refers also to the development of the practice of borrowing and lending by non-US nationals of the stock of 'real' dollars so accumulated. But there is no immediate connection between this and the persistent trade imbalances and consequent international debt explosion with which earlier chapters of this book were most concerned. The account so far explains why, if there had to be a Eurocurrency, it was more likely to be a Eurodollar than a Europound, but it does not answer the principal question, why a Eurocurrency at all.

The truth is that the modern term Eurofinance covers a number of quite separate operations which might better have been kept distinct. Eurobanks do not just receive and onlend trade surpluses to countries in deficit. They engage in all activities ranging from short-term borrowing and lending to and from multinational corporations, the placement of, and trading in, marketable bonds and the provision of longer term loans to governments and corporations, to continuous participation in foreign exchange markets. While the basic traffic has been the accepting of deposits with fixed maturity, the lending of funds with specified interest rates and maturity, and the issuing of and trading in bonds, the participating intermediaries have devised an array of instruments to meet changing conditions. Only a few need to be mentioned: syndicated loans to spread risk, floating rate bonds to match sharp fluctuations of interest rates in the deposit market, certificates of deposit to meet the liquidity needs of the interbank market rather than the non-bank participants, these being the so-called lock-up certificates of deposit, and revolving credit facilities for lenders.

Eurofinancing arrangements are now the cornerstone of international capital markets. The techniques are no longer confined to their initial European setting but permeate international financing wherever it is undertaken around the world. During the 1970s it became increasingly difficult to distinguish between Eurofinancing and other international capital transactions (Heller, 1979). In the latter years of the 1970s distinctions between the activities of US banks operating from 'off-shore' locations in the Caribbean and from their domestic locations reflected short-term convenience as much as intrinsic difference. Borrowing and lending activities are intimately linked to foreign exchange transactions, so that the partition of each operation into its various components, however desirable, might not be easy. The whole market now extends far beyond its original European location with centers open for business at almost any time in the Middle East and South East Asia as well as in Europe and the USA. The terms 'zenofinancing' and 'zenomarkets' proposed by Fritz Machlup as an alternative to 'Euro' have the merit of emphasizing the common feature of participating institutions, namely, the use of currencies other than that of the country of domicile (Machlup, 1972; McKenzie, 1976; McKinnon, 1977; Stigum, 1978).

(ii) *Necessary Distinctions*

All of this heightens the need to preserve the one essential distinction made over and over again above. Zenomarkets, just because they are zeno, do not *necessarily* cause international indebtedness to grow. They simply provide a means of handling the debt if it does grow. In sixteenth century Britain the use of foreign currencies was commonplace. The gold and silver coinage of many countries freely circulated and was readily borrowed and lent. But there is no reason why this should have been, or was, the cause of increased accumulated debt. No doubt foreign coins appeared in Britain, in the first instance, in consequence of a trade surplus. No doubt also their presence, if they were 'good' coins, might have induced some lender to stipulate repayment in the same (foreign) currency. But this, of itself, would not have *caused* there to be more borrowers or lenders than there otherwise would.

In looking at the figures below which record the growth of the Eurodollar market it should be borne in mind that what is represented is growing world debt not a growing money stock. This is true whether we are talking of the assets of Eurobanks (lending) or of their liabilities (deposits or borrowings). What we are measuring is not analogous to the value of foreign gold coins circulating in Britain in the sixteenth century. It is analogous to the value of outstanding debt which, it might have been agreed, was to be repaid in some stipulated foreign coinage rather than English silver pennies.

We could, if we had so chosen, have measured the growth of the Euromarket in terms of the average quantity of real money held by Eurobanks to conduct their transactions, including all the different kinds of transactions mentioned above. This *would* be analogous to counting, in sixteenth century Britain, the total value of foreign coins in circulation and might be an interesting statistic. To find it we would have had to look among the assets recorded in Eurobank balance sheets for dollar deposits in checking accounts in clearing banks located in the USA. The total would be small, almost negligible, compared to the total of all assets, mostly loans and bonds. No doubt the figure would show growth over time matching the growth in the value per unit of time of all Eurobank transactions; but there is no reason at all why this should match the growth of Eurodebt, that is, the total assets of Eurobanks. If debt was regularly paid off so that debtors were sometimes creditors and creditors sometimes debtors we might have a quite small total of accumulated debt with a very high value of transactions per unit of time. In this case the real money would represent a much higher proportion of total Eurobank assets and the whole system would exist on a smaller scale. Today's debt is large because debtors are always debtors and total accumulated debt is increasing. It is with debt we are concerned and it is debt which is likely to cause problems. It is for this reason that we, and most other commentators, are most concerned with the size of the accumulated debt. We turn now to the figures.

(iii)   *Market Growth*

Estimates for recent annual changes in international bank lending and bond raisings are shown in Table 4.1. They are based upon data compiled by the Bank for International Settlements (BIS); these compilations are subject to revision and varying degrees of guesswork. Estimates for international bank lending are more secure than assessments of the total financing available, shown in the last few rows of the table. The BIS cautions users of the data on repurchase and redemptions of bonds as these estimates are subject to substantial error.

The changes shown for each year are comparable in the coverage of countries and items in each of the years up to 1978. In that year Austria, Denmark and Ireland were added to the list of European reporting countries previously comprising Belgium, Luxembourg, France, Germany, Italy, Netherlands,

Table 4.1 International Lending: Domestic and Foreign Currencies and Bonds (US$ billion)

Lenders	Amounts Outstanding End of 1972	Changes in each Year Shown								Amounts Outstanding End of 1980
		1973	1974	1975	1976	1977	1978	1979	1980	
1 Banks in European countries	149.6	62.2	35.0	50.5	55.7	80.6	145.2	164.8	126.9	902.9
1a of which: in Eurocurrency	131.6	56.8	26.8	42.9	47.2	68.5	117.2	137.9	111.5	751.2
2 Banks in Canada and Japan	24.0	5.4	5.1	0.3	4.8	0.8	16.2	15.9	30.1	101.2
3 Banks in the USA	20.7	6.0	19.5	13.6	21.3	11.5	37.8	17.1	40.9	176.9
4 US branches in 'off-shore' centers	9.4	14.1	12.6	15.0	23.8	16.2	15.4	21.2	14.5	142.1
5 Gross new lending (1 to 4)	203.7	87.7	72.2	78.8	105.6	109.1	214.6	218.1	212.4	1,323.1
5a of which: in Eurocurrency (1a, 2, 4)	165.0	76.3	44.5	58.2	75.8	85.5	148.8	175.0	156.1	994.5

6 Less double-counting: redepositing among reporting banks	83.1	36.2	29.7	38.8	35.6	34.1	104.6	88.1	67.4	513.1
	120.6	51.5	42.5	40.0	70.0	75.0	110.0	130.0	145.0	810.0
7 Net new lending (5 less 6)	—	9.9	12.3	22.9	34.3	36.1	37.3	37.1	38.3	—
8 Eurobond and Foreign Bond issues	—	2.5	3.0	3.3	4.3	5.1	8.3	9.6	9.3	—
9 Less redemption and repurchases	—	7.4	9.3	19.5	30.0	31.0	29.0	27.5	29.0	—
10 Total Net New Bonds	—	97.6	84.5	101.7	139.9	145.2	251.9	255.2	250.7	—
11 Total New Bank and Bond Financing (5 and 8)	—	58.9	51.8	59.5	100.0	106.0	139.0	157.5	174.0	—
12 Total Net New Financing (7 and 10)	—	2.5	2.1	2.5	3.5	4.0	6.0	7.5	8.0	—
13 Less double-counting: banks purchasing bonds										

Source: Bank for International Settlements, various annual reports. Row 5a and 11 are interpretations of BIS data.

Sweden, Switzerland and the UK. In addition there was a change in coverage of domestic currency assets held externally in France and the UK and custody items in the USA. The change in 1979 is based upon the revised coverage.

The estimates explore the sources of international funding amongst European, North American and Japanese banks including the affiliates of US banks in certain 'off-shore' locations. Coverage is not complete in that some new centers, such as Bahrain and Singapore, are not included at all or only partially. Nevertheless the estimates do take account of the great bulk of transactions; the newer centers remain relatively small.

All international lending by banks and similar institutions is covered in the estimates. Thus the series includes not only those activities based upon deposits drawn from sources external to the country in which the financing institution is located, the feature that typifies Eurofinancing, but also the more traditional forms of direct foreign lending by banks in the currency of the country in which they are located. An important reason for offering this wider series is the apparent interlocking of lending in domestic and foreign currencies. Foreign lending from national capital markets may fund syndicated loans in Eurocurrencies (Solomon, 1979, p. 5). This possibility pinpoints one problem of measuring total activity in circumstances where double counting is almost inevitable.

The estimates for international bank lending are divided into four main categories: the European banks with a sub-grouping for Eurocurrency transactions, Japanese and Canadian banks, direct lending by US banks and lending by off-shore affiliates of those banks. Comparison of the types of activities by European banks is straightforward. With banks in Canada and Japan the great bulk of lending is in foreign currencies; their activities are the same as the Eurofinancing operations of the European banks.

Interpretation of the two series for lending by US banks and their off-shore affiliates is more difficult. Off-shore financing is Eurofinancing; certainly deposits are attracted from an outside source for lending to borrowers elsewhere. Yet in important respects this identification is not complete. US authorities, by imposing reserve requirements for which the banks do not receive interest and pursuing interest rate policies which open obvious differentials with those applying in international capital markets, gave incentives to the expansion of affiliates using funds outside national jurisdiction. Hence lending by these affiliates may be interpreted as a substitute for direct lending by financial institutions in the USA. Support for this interpretation is furnished by the clear evidence of expansion of direct lending following the authorities' decision in August 1978 to remove reserve requirements on deposits by foreign banks at US commercial banks. With the reversal of this decision on 6 October 1979, American banks have again made a switch in their activities between the two locations. Comparisons may be made between rows 4 and 5 in Table 4.1.

Recent years have seen a relative decline in the contribution of bond issues to the flow of new financing. The gross value of new bond issues has remained stable over the last four years at a time when other forms of lending were rising swiftly. When account is taken of repurchases and redemptions and the possibilities for institutions in the Eurofinance markets to take up bond issues, which would count as lending in Table 4.1 row 13, the net value of new bond issues has declined in significance. The offering of floating rate issues does not appear to have reversed this trend during 1980.

This outcome is not surprising in light of the disturbed nature of foreign exchange markets, especially with the dollar, from the final quarter of 1977 onwards. Big jumps in interest rates on Eurodollar deposits during this period created an inverse yield curve for dollar-denominated Eurobonds. This feature, in conjunction with the exchange risks when holding such bonds, meant a diminished interest in new issues. New bond issues had become relatively less attractive than direct loans for most of the period between 1976 and 1979 as borrowers were able to extract better terms and compress margins over LIBOR, the most favorable deposit rate. Another reason is that a bond placement involves a much greater market test than a direct loan from one or a syndicate of financial intermediaries. This would be important to borrowers already heavily in debt in foreign capital markets at a time when questions of risk have become a matter for common concern.

Eurofinancing institutions have provided the great bulk of funds by direct lending. In Table 4.1 distinctions are made between gross and net estimates of new lending between 1973 and 1980, the difference being interbank depositing. During those eight years the total value of both gross and net lending has risen about six and a half times. Although the annual patterns are not uniform and vary between the series, including that for Eurocurrencies in row 5a, the variability is only in the rate of expansion.

In Table 4.2, BIS estimates are shown for the amounts outstanding as direct loans for the same period. Other estimates than those provided by the BIS have been calculated. Most familiar are those from Morgan Guaranty, having a somewhat wider coverage taking into account some of the newer centers not fully incorporated in the BIS series (Weatherstone, 1979). These alternative series are shown, gross and net, in the final two rows of Table 4.2. They reveal a comparable pattern of change throughout the period under review but a higher overall growth in the value of lending. As the net new lending series from Morgan Guaranty rises more slowly than the gross series, they point to a larger interbank activity than is indicated in the BIS series.

The European centers have been dominant throughout the 1970s. Comparisons of relative contributions from different centers is only possible for the gross series; there is little information on interbank deposit activity outside London. The Europeans provide 73.4 percent of gross outstandings at the end of 1972 and 69.9 percent at the end of 1979. Amongst the European centers London maintained its dominant position with nearly 45 percent of all activity. Next in importance was

Table 4.2 International Bank Lending: Amounts of Loans Outstanding (US$ billion)

Lenders	Amounts Outstanding at End of Each Year								
	1972	1973	1974	1975	1976	1977	1978[a]	1979	1980
1 Banks in European countries	149.6	211.8	246.8	297.3	353.0	433.6	611.4	776.0	902.9
1a of which: in Eurocurrency	131.6	188.4	215.2	455.4	302.6	371.1	502.0	639.7	751.2
2 Banks in Canada and Japan	24.0	29.4	34.5	34.2	39.0	39.8	56.0	71.1	101.2
3 Banks in the USA	20.7	26.7	46.2	59.8	81.1	92.6	119.2	136.0	176.9
4 US branches in 'off-shore' centers	9.4	23.5	36.1	51.1	74.9	91.1	106.5	127.6	142.1
5 Gross lending	203.7	291.4	363.6	442.4	548.0	657.1	893.1	1,110.7	1,323.1
5a of which: in Eurocurrency (1a, 2, 4)	164.0	241.3	385.8	340.7	416.5	502.0	664.5	838.6	994.5
6 Less double-counting: redepositing among reporting banks	83.1	119.3	149.0	187.8	223.4	257.5	358.1	445.7	513.1
7 Not lending	120.6	172.1	214.6	254.6	324.6	399.6	535.0	665.0	810.0
8 Eurocurrency Market:									
a Gross	205	310	390	480	590	725	930	1,190	1,470
b Net	110	160	215	250	310	380	485	600	735

Notes: [a]Series II estimates comparable with 1979 and later years. Series I estimates for 1978 comparable with earlier years were 611.4, 502.0, 56.0, 130.8, 106.5, 904.7, 664.7, 364.7, 540.

Source: Rows 1–7, Bank for International Settlements, various annual reports and reviews.
Row 8, Morgan Guaranty Trust Company, World Financial Markets, various issues.

Paris with about 15 percent. Luxembourg and Belgium follow, reflecting the increasing role of the Deutschmark in total transactions. Unfortunately, the lack of data on the foreign activities of German banks does not permit a reasonable assessment of their performance; the Bundesbank (1980, p. 50) admits to reporting on only 40 percent of their transactions.

During the period the US banks, directly or through their 'off-shore' affiliates, increased their share from 14.8 percent at the end of 1972 to 23.7 percent at the end of 1979. Thus only in 1978 and 1979 did the Japanese banks and, to a much lesser extent, the Canadian banks begin to recover what had always been a modest share in the markets. But assessing relative positions is always made difficult by the double-counting and the diversion of funds through different centers. Much of the Canadian activity in the 1960s and early 1970s would have been a reflection of the techniques employed by American banks to avoid the regulatory restraints imposed by their authorities. Furthermore the 'off-shore' affiliates were often funded from the USA and Europe.

The rise in the American share appears to coincide with the abandoning of many regulatory restraints. The considerable rise in direct lending by US affiliated banks during 1978 suggests one explanation for the strains experienced by the dollar in foreign exchange markets at that time. One reason for this was the relative attractiveness of foreign lending when domestic interest rates were lower than in dollar-denominated Eurocurrency and major American banks were losing their share of domestic banking business (Wallich, 1978, p. 9).

There is little dispute about the rapidity with which Euro-financing has grown through the past decade. Hence argument about the precise measure of change is misplaced, particularly when it directs attention away from more fundamental issues. Some structural features do, however, warrant consideration.

(iv)   *Market Structures*

It is instructive to distinguish four separate elements in zeno-finance taken as a whole. First there is an interbank market in which the participating financial institutions make deposits and borrow amongst themselves. Estimates in Tables 4.1 and 4.2 show how large this activity has grown in the past decade. If the Morgan Guaranty estimates are a reasonable guide then the BIS series understates its size. The typical transaction in the interbank market appears to be short term.

The second element covers the acceptance of deposits from, and the granting of loans to, financial institutions not participating in the market and to governments and companies. These transactions involve loans for longer periods than is usually the case in the interbank market.

The third element is the so-called Eurobond market in which placements provide an alternative means for the financing of government and company spending to that offered by direct lending from participating banks. In this case there is a market test for the relative standing of borrowers as well as the currencies in which the bonds are denominated.

Finally, there is the foreign exchange market in which participating institutions, borrowers and lenders establish the relativities for the currencies in which transactions are undertaken. In a most important sense, a foreign exchange element is embodied each time a deposit, loan or bond placement is negotiated.

Controversy surrounds the role of the interbank market (Frydl, 1978–9). The common, though false, belief that Euro-bank deposits are in some sense 'money' as well as debt is not usually carried over to interbank debt. There seems to be a willingness to recognize that money lent by bank A to bank B cannot be spent (or lent for spending) twice over even though two entries labeled 'deposits' are visible in the accounts of the banking system. This might be thought strange in view of the vehemence with which it is quite ordinarily argued that when a loan between persons A and B is negotiated through a financial intermediary both A's deposit in the financial intermediary *and* the intermediary's check on its checking bank, now passed to B, can be spent freely on goods.

The truth is of course that money is money and debt is debt while neither is both. The idea that Eurodeposits owned by non-banks is money while Eurodeposits owned by banks is not underlies the claim that counting interbank deposits is 'double' counting. If we are trying to count money *all* Eurodeposits should be excluded. If, on the other hand, we are counting debt then interbank debt must be included.

It is true that financial intermediaries are efficient in the sense that they probably speed up the process of matching savers with borrowers. No doubt also the existence of intermediaries gives confidence, provides insurance, and keeps interest rates down. But intermediaries do not allow saving to be spent twice over and for that reason should not be supposed to have any effect upon the supply of 'true' money.

The argument that interbank debt is truly debt, with its concomitant problems, deserves some development. First there are loans to bank borrowers at longer maturity than for corresponding deposits so that there are risk issues involved. Secondly, the interbank market offers a means of shifting risk to other participants so there is risk spreading. Thirdly, the variability in interbank activity to other lending activities evident in 1975 after the Herstatt failure, and then again in 1978, suggests a widespread use of the interbank market to cover risk arising from foreign exchange instability, and from lending itself and mismatching of portfolios of deposits and assets. Fourthly, there is the very real question of the capacity of the interbank market to provide the ready liquidity of assets and deposits when there is no direct access to a lender of last resort. A corollary to this question is whether or not the institutions participating in direct lending are banks in any real sense.

For those borrowers outside the interbank market — the so-called non-bank users — there is a substantial mismatching of maturities. The most comprehensive evidence is from the

London market which, given its share of total activity, is a reasonable guide to the overall position. Other centers of any size would not, by the laws of competition, be in a position to adopt different market strategies. Non-bank users take about 25 percent of all loans, including the interbank market, with between 55 and 60 percent having a maturity of more than one year. For banks outside the UK, loans with that maturity comprise about 12 percent of all loans while deposits with similar maturity were 3.5 to 4.5 percent of total deposits in recent years. Some BIS data is available on maturities outside the reporting area of Europe, Canada, Japan and the USA and its off-shore facilities. At the end of June 1979 liabilities (deposits) were recorded as $224.2 billion while loans (assets) are shown as $320.6 billion. Some $147.4 billion had a maturity of over one year; this is 45.97 percent of total assets. The proportion for maturities over two years was 37.07 percent. The general position for these borrowers is shown in Table 4.3 though the estimates understate the maturities over one year because of limited information from some major lenders such as France and the USA. Estimates for some of the countries shown may not be complete.

A major demand for liquidity could not be met by the non-bank borrowers. About 25 percent of loans outstanding have a maturity over one year with most of that having a maturity of more than two years. This compares with the bulk of funds, say around 90 percent, in the interbank market being placed with a maturity of six months or less. Any 'unwinding' of the interbank market to gain access to money would pose enormous strains on major participating institutions whatever the lending policy of individual banks.

What the estimates in Table 4.3 also reveal is the concentration of borrowing amongst relatively few countries. The fourteen countries shown separately take up more than half the loans and have a somewhat higher proportion than average committed with longer maturities. If the evidence from the London market alone is any guide then most of these maturities would be for more than three years.

Table 4.3   *Liabilities, Assets and Maturities External to Euro-financing Centers — end June 1980*

US$ billion Regions and Countries	Liabilities (Deposits)	Assets (Loans) Over 1 year Maturity		
		Total	Amount	% of Total
1 Developed countries not in BIS Reporting Area	45.6	81.6	41.5	50.9
2 Eastern Europe	12.3	57.8	27.4	47.4
of which: East Germany	2.2	9.7	4.6	47.4
Hungary	0.8	7.8	3.8	48.7
Poland	0.7	15.8	8.3	52.5
USSR	6.3	12.4	5.7	46.0
3 Latin America	53.6	139.8	72.2	51.6
of which: Argentina	7.2	17.3	7.7	44.5
Brazil	5.0	41.0	24.7	60.2
Mexico	8.3	34.7	20.0	57.6
Venezuela	15.7	20.8	8.1	38.9
4 Middle East	126.4	32.2	8.2	25.5
of which: Iran	7.7	5.6	3.2	57.1
United Emirates	5.4	5.6	2.0	35.7
5 Africa	19.0	29.6	13.0	43.9
of which: Algeria	4.3	9.3	5.4	58.1
6 Asia	35.0	45.5	18.5	40.7
of which: Indonesia	7.5	5.9	3.1	52.5
S. Korea	2.7	14.3	5.4	37.8
Philippines	3.2	8.2	3.4	41.5
7 TOTAL	291.9	386.4	180.8	46.8
of which individual countries listed:	77.0	208.4	105.4	50.6
%	26.4	53.9	58.3	—

Source: Bank for International Settlements, *Maturity Distribution of International Bank Lending*, December 1980.

No direct evidence is available relating to shifts in structure participation and maturity in the interbank market. However, there is some indirect evidence on its role as a hedging market with respect to risk. The interbank market has adapted, some might say 'distorted', the certificate of deposit (CD) to meet certain needs. Whereas a CD is usually issued by a participating intermediary to a non-bank customer seeking real liquidity because that instrument can be readily negotiated, many participants have bought and sold them amongst themselves on the understanding that they would not be traded. Hence the name lock-up CDs. In this way the appearance of liquidity is preserved while the rate may be slightly below the comparable maturity for a time deposit. The volume of this type of CD is in dispute though claims have been advanced that they may amount to 50 percent of all CDs. Thus impressions of liquidity can be exaggerated.

This raises again the crucial issue referred to many times above. What constitutes liquidity in the interbank market or, indeed, in any aspect of Eurofinancing? Where banks own foreign currency deposits in other Eurobanks in what sense are these deposits really liquid? The owner of a Eurodeposit cannot draw checks against it in the designated currency, or any currency. The asset they own is no more than an obligation to pay on maturity in a foreign currency. To get the foreign currency to meet a maturing deposit or CD the bank liable must buy that currency in the foreign exchange market or have a balance at a commercial bank or a central bank. Only then can there exist access to the necessary foreign exchange. In this way the transactions of Eurofinancing institutions are analogous to those of a non-bank financial intermediary in a national monetary system.

Accordingly, the actions of governments and central banks in their management of exchange rates bear directly upon the workings of the interbank market. The market interacts with the official interventions. Monetary authorities' interventions to stabilize currency rates add to the funds in the markets as swap arrangements and the like work to support those currencies under pressure. And the actions of the participating institutions in matching spot and forward exchange commitments to secure covered positions for their forward transactions can bring in more funds. Some part of the explanation for the increase in direct lending by American banks in 1978 is to be found in the workings of Eurofinance markets. In the latter part of 1978 heavy forward sales of dollars brought a large premium for strong currencies, such as the Deutschmark. Eurofinancing institutions sold dollars spot for those currencies to match forward commitments. To finance this they borrowed dollars in the USA, generating a monetary capital outflow from the USA. It was the availability of bank credit in the USA which sustained the outflow. When monetary policy tightened in November 1978, the dollar stopped being under pressure.

Thus the interbank market holds a central position in the workings of Eurofinance markets. It is intimately linked to the liquidity of the overall market and reflects the foreign exchange ramifications of all transactions. At the same time it responds to, and influences the availability of, loans to non-bank users and the prices required for that access. In a most important sense it is the wholesale market for other activities.

As noted earlier in this section, borrowers outside Eurofinance centers gain access to funds at maturities much longer than the terms on which funds are supplied. This mismatching of maturities bears upon the means by which the participants earn profits. The greater the mismatch the greater the risk for individual firms and the market as a whole.

(v) *Sources of Finance*

Although the measure of expansion of the Euromarket revealed in Tables 4.1 and 4.2 is a measure of Eurodebt there can be no increase in debt without a flow of money. Someone must save, or print money, before anyone else can borrow. Yet institutions other than banks provide only about 14 percent of funds in the London market. The balance must come from financial institutions outside Eurofinance markets, which receive savings or are checking banks or central banks able to create new money.

The interbank market has an intermediary role rather than an initiatory function.

Elsewhere in this book we have intimated that the principal source of Eurofunds must be continuing trade surpluses. In short, deficit countries that print or borrow money to exchange into Eurocurrencies to support trade imbalances pass on that money in exchange for goods to surplus countries who deposit their earnings in a Eurobank. This is more likely to show up in flow of funds data as lending by commercial and central banks to the Euromarket, though it does not entirely rule out the possibility of non-bank lending. What are the facts?

One set of estimates was made on the sources of funds to the Eurocurrency market about the middle of 1975 (Mayer, 1976). This calculation put the proportion coming from central banks at 25 percent. Given the size of the market at that time, this would amount to about US$76 billion. This information suggests a somewhat different view of the sources of funds than the data for the London market. Non-bank participants might be relatively more important than the London data implies even allowing for the uncertainty of how to classify funds coming from trustee accounts managed by Swiss commercial banks; that source yielded about 30 percent of liabilities or about $91 billion in 1975. All this implies a need for care in arguing from the detailed information on one lender market to the Eurofinancing institutions as a whole, as is to be expected from the theory of the balance of payments.

If estimates for the role of central banks and similar agencies continued to be applicable at the end of 1978, then that source would be providing some US$165 billion. What evidence is there to support that possibility? One authoritative comment reads (Wallich, 1979):

> Moreover, G-10 central banks with some exceptions do not maintain deposits in the Euro-markets. Consequently, it is the smaller central banks that may, and recently have, engaged in some switching from one currency to another, especially out of dollars. The deposits of the non-G-10 central banks in the

Euro-market, therefore, must be added to the deposits of non-banks in order to arrive at the volume of funds capable of switching readily. These smaller central bank holdings are estimated at about $105 billion . . .

No guess is made of the exceptions to the restricted participation of the G-10 countries. However, there has been a gentlemen's agreement amongst the central banks in these countries to restrict their activities in Eurocurrency markets since the Smithsonian Agreement of 1971. That feature appears as the one permanent and effective remnant from those negotiations. In passing it is of course relevant to wonder in what sense foreign currency reserves of central banks not held in other central banks can exist without being invested *somewhere*. They may feed the Euromarket indirectly even though not directly deposited by central banks.

Evidently there is widespread use of foreign exchange reserves, however indirectly, for the financing of deficits accruing to many countries. This conclusion is inescapable. Estimates by Morgan Guaranty (1980) show central bank deposits in the Eurocurrency market rising by $50 billion between the end of 1975 and the end of 1978 when they amounted to $120 billion with a further increase of $35 billion in 1979.

There has been a sustained effort to reduce Eurofinancing from official sources. However, the growing total of foreign exchange reserves placed in the Eurofinancing markets by central banks, other than those of the advanced industrial countries, has been and remains a major long-term source of funds. There is no reason for thinking that present international arrangements can achieve a slowing down of this expansionary thrust so long as major imbalances exist in world trade.

Central bank foreign exchange deposits become important only when they are onlent to provide additional foreign exchange balances from outside the Eurofinance market to the participating intermediaries. Central banks, or monetary authorities, acting in this way are, in effect, shifting their foreign exchange reserves from claims on other central banks, most often the Federal Reserve Bank of New York, to claims on banks. Participating institutions gain balances in New York or elsewhere, which so become available to borrowing countries in trade deficit.

For purposes of illustration, discussion proceeds on the basis of the US dollar. The trade surplus of any country accepting payment in dollars shows itself as a dollar balance in New York, embodied in the foreign exchange reserves of the surplus country. An institution seeking dollars to lend to a borrower in a third country can offer an interest rate sufficient to attract those funds. The initial act of borrowing changes the ownership of the dollar balances in New York; there may be a shift in location from one New York bank to another. The Eurofinancing institution has increased its liabilities balanced initially by an asset, the dollar holdings in New York. When the Eurofinancing institution loans the dollars to the borrower, the asset shifts from a dollar deposit in New York to a dollar-denominated loan. The borrower then holds the dollar balance which may be used in a variety of ways: for payment of imports, repayment of previous loans, accumulation in private foreign exchange holdings, selling to the borrower's central bank in order to finance domestic activity, further participation in Eurofinancing activities, or increasing liquidity.

In all circumstances there is no change in the total amount of dollars held in New York. However, there are increased dollar-denominated liabilities and assets in the Eurofinancing institutions representing debt not money. The types and extent of transactions help explain the variations in the margin observed between the gross and net series of amounts outstanding in international capital markets estimated by the Bank for International Settlements and summarised in Tables 4.1 and 4.2.

The growth of international debt can continue without new money creation anywhere. On the other hand, if governments *do* create new money it is as likely as not that some of this will find its way into the hands of Eurobanks where it may serve to generate even greater trade deficits and, ipso facto, an even faster growing total of international debt.

References

Deutsche Bundesbank (1980), *Report for the Year 1979*, 17 April.

Frydl, E. J. (1978–79), 'The debate over regulating the Eurocurrency markets', *Federal Reserve Bank of New York Quarterly Review*, vol. 4, no. 4, Winter, pp. 11–20.

Heller, H. Robert (1979), *Statement*, Joint Hearing of Subcommittees of the Committee on Banking, Finance and Urban Affairs, US House of Representatives, 27 June.

Machlup, F. (1972), 'Euro-dollars, once again', *Banca Nazionale del Lavoro Quarterly Review*, no. 101, June, pp. 119–37.

Mayer, H. W. (1976). 'The BIS concept of the Eurocurrency market', *Euromoney*, May, pp. 60–6.

McKenzie, G. W. (1976), *The Economics of the Euro-Currency-System*, (London: Macmillan), p. 141.

McKinnon, R. I. (1977), *The Eurocurrency Market*, Essays in International Finance, No. 125, December (Princeton: International Finance Section, Princeton University), p. 40.

Morgan Guaranty (1980), *World Financial Markets*, November.

Solomon, A. M. (1979), *Statement*, Joint Hearing of Subcommittees of the Committee on Banking, Finance and Urban Affairs, US House of Representatives, 12 July.

Stigum, M. (1978), *The Money Market: Myth, Reality and Practice* (Homewood, Ill.: Dow Jones-Irwin).

Wallich, H. (1979), 'Euro-markets and U.S. monetary growth', *Journal of Commerce*, May 1 and 2, transcript version.

Wallich, H. (1978), 'International lending and the Euromarkets', Euromarkets Conference sponsored by the *Financial Times*, London, 9 May 1978.

Weatherstone, D. (1979), *Statement*, Joint Hearing of Subcommittees of the Committee on Banking, Finance and Urban Affairs, US House of Representatives, 26 June.

5 Market Instability: Risk and Speculation

(i) *Eurodollar Market Efficiency?*

The Eurodollar market as a whole is frequently praised for its efficiency and, in a sense, this epithet is justified. If the object of the exercise had been simply to establish a collective institution where money might be bought and sold at a common price, where information is readily accessible at a moment's notice and where the special needs of borrowers and lenders, however peculiar, could always be met, at a price, then the Eurodollar market must be judged to be near perfect. And from the point of view of participating banks this *is* the beginning and the end of the matter.

The coordination of international capital transactions is complete. Communication and cooperation is almost instantaneous. Huge sums of money can be quickly mobilized, currency exchanges effected and the whole placed wherever it is in demand, in what would seem to be the twinkling of an eye. It is fashionable to argue that what has been achieved is 'a more effective use of money' or to claim a 'startling capacity to adapt to the changing needs of depositors and borrowers', so as to 'solve' the problem of 'financing' international trade.

But what can these words possibly mean? A 'more effective use of money' is a phrase that simply indicates, if it indicates anything at all, that less time is needed to match lenders and borrowers. But this, by itself, does not imply that money circulates any faster than it otherwise would. It simply means that the borrower is holding the money rather than the lender, with a consequent obligation to pay interest. It does not follow that the borrower will spend the money any quicker since it was borrowed for a definite purpose which need not be affected by the speed or simplicity of the borrowing operation. Nor is it true, even if there were some partial speeding up of the monetary circulation, that there would *necessarily* be some advantage to society in this. A large amount of money circulating slowly is no more costly than a small amount of money circulating rapidly. The advantage to the lender is, of course, obvious. No one wishes to hold idle money when it can earn interest. But the extra interest is paid by the borrower. The advantage to the lender is offset by the cost to the borrower. There is no prima facie case that any *new* borrower will emerge just because of the speed at which lenders and borrowers can be matched. Lenders are generated by not spending income (or by money printing). Spenders are generated by intentions to spend more than current income. The speed at which the market discovers and matches the two classes is less relevant than some writers suppose.

'Capacity to adapt to the changing needs of depositors and borrowers' is a vastly different matter. What this usually means is that the Euromarket is adept at finding means to make a bad lending proposition look like a good one. However poor the prospects of the borrower and however doubtful his capacity to repay, some way will be found to persuade the owner of cash to accept the risk, usually by hiding it. Conversely, whenever a surplus of funds appears the market will produce a borrower and close ranks to ensure that the lender will feel safe.

All of this does affect the real economy. Borrowers and lenders can be generated who might not otherwise be borrowers or lenders. Money can be channeled into the wrong projects. Lenders can be induced to pass on funds to finance spending that they would not think of supporting if they knew the facts, and if, knowing all the facts, they were required to carry the risk unsupported by an underwriting bank. In consequence the rate of interest is maintained higher than it otherwise would be, crowding out, perhaps, more productive (and safer) spending elsewhere.

Nor can underwriting banks serve as proxies for discriminating and self-interested lenders who, precisely because of their self-interest, are bound to ensure that their funds are safely spent on socially desirable projects. The reason for this is simple. Banks do *not* refuse deposits, and having once accepted a deposit they are bound to find a borrower at once or lose money. This overriding need has encouraged the banking community to agree to support one another to a remarkable and dangerous degree. The greater is the belief in the system the greater are the risks that banks feel able to take. And the greater the risks they take, the more misdirected are the funds they handle. At the same time the more widespread are the agreements designed to undo the consequences of bad investments the more likely it is that a collapse, if it came, would be on a grand scale.

One consequence of all this is the discovery by countries in trade deficit that they do not, after all, need the services of the International Monetary Fund. All the foreign currency they require may be borrowed from Eurobanks. Table 5.1 shows all too clearly the role of the Eurodollar market in sustaining the very same trade maladjustments that allow the Eurobanks to continue to grow. Private money flows, themselves dominated by Eurobank underwriting, have provided the bulk of trade deficit finance. Official multilateral institutions, the International Monetary Fund and the World Bank (IBRD) have played only a modest part limited mainly to the developing economies not exporting oil.

One crumb of comfort may perhaps be drawn from evidence emerging in the past two years or more of the growing influence of IMF judgments upon Euromarket lending terms and conditions. Traditionally, and indeed essentially, the IMF has undertaken reviews of the effectiveness of economic policies in countries subject to severe problems in their balance of payments. There is now reason to believe that, to some degree, participating financial institutions in the Eurodollar market look to the IMF for guidance. This does not, however, suggest that there is no need for further concern. The trade equilibrating mechanism shows no signs yet of reasserting itself, nor does the newly proclaimed concern of the Eurodollar market

Table 5.1 *Financing Requirements of Deficit Countries, 1976 to 1978 (US$ billion)*

	1976	1977	1978
1 All deficit countries other than the USA	77	71	75
a Current account deficits	72	65	68
b Foreign exchange reserve changes	5	6	7
2 OECD countries other than the USA	33	35	28
a Current account deficits	37	33	23
3 OPEC countries	2	4	9
a Current account deficits	2	5	14
4 Non-oil exporting developing economies	29	23	29
a Current account deficits	22	18	22
5 Other countries	13	9	9
a Current account deficits	11	9	9
6 Sources of financing			
a Official flows (net) of which	19	13	15
(i) International Monetary Fund	6	0	0
(ii) Multilateral financing (not IMF)	5	6	7
(iii) Bilateral credits	9	8	8
b Private flows of which	66	61	67
(i) Net indebtedness to banks	39	29	39
(ii) Bond issues	17	17	14
(ii) Net direct to portfolio investment	10	15	14
c Total	85	74	82
7 Balancing item (6c−1)	7	2	7

Source: These estimates are taken from the tables attached to testimony by Honorable Anthony M. Solomon, then Under Secretary of the Treasury for Monetary Affairs (Solomon, 1979b).

with national policies appear statistically to have had much effect. The world financial situation continues to be one of high and disquieting risk.

(ii) *Elements of Risk*

Risk in Eurofinance markets comprises the usual features associated with lending in any market, together with sovereign or country risk when lending involves transactions across national boundaries (Aliber, 1978). Given the nature of Euro-financing, sovereign risk applies to the great bulk of loans to final users. Commercial risk elements should be familiar: first, the credit risk associated with the ability of borrowers to repay; secondly, the ability of lending institutions to manage assets and liabilities in ways that will avoid liquidity problems; and, thirdly, the risks associated with the potential variability of interest rates and foreign exchange relativities.

In many respects, markets commonly embody techniques for containing risk. The comprehensive spot and forward markets in foreign exchange allow financial institutions to hedge their exchange risks. Ronald McKinnon (1977) has drawn attention to the intimate links between lending and exchange operations. Similarly, loans are designed to curtail the risk associated with interest rate changes by providing for periodic adjustments based upon shifts in the London Inter-bank Offered Rate (LIBOR). Moreover, some loans provide for flexibility in maturity dates, thus allowing some further adaptations of the maturity structure of asset portfolios. In this way some aspects of commercial risk are diminished.

Sovereign risk is a quite separate matter. Government guarantees of loans to domestic banks and other borrowing institutions do not bear upon sovereign risk, being rather linked to reducing margins for commercial risk. Sovereign risk concerns national capacities to fund debt service requirements on all loans, official or otherwise, owing to foreign lenders. Additionally, there is the possibility of legislative actions, such as nationalization, involving inadequate provisions for repayment of loans. Problems arising over compensation for the seizure of equity capital do not bear directly on lending though the repercussions for lending would be clear.

We have already commented above upon one aspect of sovereign risk, namely, IMF supervision of the national policies of governments seeking to increase an already heavy foreign indebtedness, and the linking of such supervision with the terms of further Eurodollar borrowing. But this approach to sovereign risk has yet to be tested. Lengthening of maturities on loans suggests extensions well beyond the reach of agreements negotiated under the auspices of the IMF. Nor is there a basis for judging the impact when conditions laid down are not fully implemented by the particular national government. There seem to be few substitutions for an effective private assessment of commercial and sovereign risks. At best negotiations by the IMF can provide no more than a modest mitigating influence. It is hard to know whether the existence of conditional arrangements has so far influenced the lending flow for good or for ill.

(iii)   *Experience with Risk*

What of Eurofinancing behavior in relation to risk? The market appears to reflect a judgment that LIBOR is akin to a risk-free borrowing (or deposit) provision. This is implicit in the frequent reference to the risk-free character of interbank borrowings. This stance must be questioned. The interbank market is not a closed shop; it supplies a net flow of funds to the 'final users' or non-bank borrowers. In this respect LIBOR does not approximate a risk-free rate structure. Thus the capacity to liquify interbank funding depends upon the liquidity and debt servicing capacity of the final non-bank borrower. Hence the netting out of interbank assets and liabilities is scarcely justified when risk is the subject of enquiry. Accordingly, risk elements in Eurofinance markets are real, and much more significant than individual participating institutions are likely to judge. However, there is a greater awareness now than in the mid-1970s of the problems arising when lending is concentrated amongst relatively few countries.

One feature, which might be considered offsetting, is the extent to which central banks in the main Eurofinancing centers are committed to supporting their participating commercial banks. Various arrangements of an informal nature, sometimes described as 'Gentlemen's Agreements', abound in this sphere with understandings about the ways participating institutions work in different areas of the market (Andreas, 1979; Solomon, 1979a). However indirectly, there exist arrangements, inaugurated in 1974, providing what is tantamount to 'lender of last resort' facilities. Again, the concerted support by central banks of foreign exchange markets when stabilizing currency relativities frequently puts funds into Eurofinance markets just as they did on the planet Htrae (see Chapter 3). In this way liquidity strains bearing upon the liabilities of participating institutions are relieved.

Hard evidence on risk is scanty. Discussion is hampered by lack of information on the stability of lending activities, even though claims are made that losses in 1976–77 on foreign lending by commercial banks in the USA were less than those on domestic loans (Wallich, 1978, p. 4). Comparison with the domestic market is deceptive in view of the implications of loan failure in the international setting. The 'rolling-over' of loans is the accepted device for postponing the consequences of inability to repay debts. Reneging on debt obligations would affect all loans to the country concerned with implications for the status of all participating institutions as well as freezing new loan possibilities. In effect all lending institutions, private, public and multilateral, have an interest in anticipating and preventing debt failure. But this seems not to discourage risk taking. The apparent stagnation in Eurobond financing during 1978 and 1979 is indicative of a shift from a financing arrangement subject to regular market tests through offerings on major markets towards those supported more by hope and faith. There has been greater reliance on various forms of direct lending from banks, individually or in some form of syndicate or consortium. The general features exhibited in lending during the past two years have shown a narrowing of margins over the cost of funds.

Limited evidence on general lending arrangements is shown in Table 5.2 for the final quarter of each calendar year between 1973 and 1978. The spread or margin is the interest rate over the LIBOR base. What is evident are the very easy conditions

Table 5.2 Spreads and Maturities of Eurocurrency Loans (Fourth Quarter of Year Shown)

	1973	1974	1975	1976	1977	1978
1 Non-Oil Developing Economies						
a Weighted mean spreads (%)	1.21	1.38	1.65	1.87	1.77	1.06
b Weighted mean maturities (years)	10.84	7.53	5.44	5.14	7.31	9.79
2 OPEC						
a Weighted mean spreads (%)	1.29	–	1.67	1.34	1.59	1.11
b Weighted mean maturities (years)	7.27	–	5.66	6.95	5.48	8.59
3 Eastern Europe						
a Weighted mean spreads (%)	0.61	–	1.49	1.29	1.16	0.73
b Weighted mean maturities (years)	8.81	–	5.54	5.50	6.00	6.71
4 Small OECD						
a Weighted mean spreads (%)	0.95	1.31	1.58	1.37	1.09	0.72
b Weighted mean maturities (years)	9.14	5.84	6.52	5.23	6.76	8.48
5 Large OECD						
a Weighted mean spreads (%)	0.67	1.14	1.62	1.29	1.04	0.56
b Weighted mean maturities (years)	8.42	4.93	5.00	5.35	5.36	8.33
6 Total						
a Weighted mean spreads (%)	0.87	1.33	1.63	1.58	1.48	0.83
b Unweighted mean spreads (%)	0.97	1.30	1.67	1.56	1.41	0.88
c Weighted mean maturities (years)	8.88	7.01	5.63	5.61	6.79	8.88
d Unweighted mean maturities (years)	9.39	6.66	5.57	5.69	6.28	8.66
e Standard deviation of spreads (%)	0.43	0.29	0.21	0.34	0.39	0.26

Source: Federal Reserve Board.

prevailing in the Eurofinance markets during 1973. Loan maturities were long while the average spread was low. This would have reflected a relatively weak demand for funding. A speedy reversal came following the rise in crude oil prices. The supply of funds to Euromarkets expanded, but demand for loans accelerated owing to the balance of payments deficits confronting many countries. Market tightness was further exaggerated by the failures of two participating institutions, Herstatt and Franklin National; in both cases foreign exchange misjudgments appear to lie at the heart of their collapse. But since the middle of 1977 market conditions have eased mainly owing to an increasing flow of funds. The effect was initially to extend average maturities and then reduce average spreads. During 1979 and 1980, for which comparable data is not yet available, there have been more rapid switches in margins and maturities.

With loans to final users, the market reveals considerable flexibility. This flexibility is seen in both maturity transformation and variation of spreads, the one not being independent of the other. The variability of average maturity and average spread over regions also appears to diminish with the tightening of the market but the evidence is not conclusive. A characteristic of the market is for spreads over LIBOR to shift up and down for all borrowers in contrast to what happens in efficient domestic capital markets where increased perceptions of risk lead to a widening of the spread within which loans are concluded. However, the drawing of parallels between domestic and international markets ignores a quite specific additional element amongst the factors bearing upon transactions, namely, the significance of sovereign risk. A justification for the general upward shift of interest rates might be that, in times of heavy need for international funding, there is a general rise in the risk of national default or delay in repayment owing to the rising debt service ratio, but such an explanation is hardly convincing.

This suggests three possibilities. First, the participating financial institutions resort to rationing loans in tight market conditions. Secondly, syndication and consortium arrangements for loans can only be provided by a relatively few firms in relation to the needs of final users. This implies lending activities exhibiting characteristics often associated with oligopoly in goods markets. This contrasts with the interbank market and its associated brokers, which, with many participants, is an efficient wholesale market. In so far as the interbank market is intimately linked to foreign exchange transactions known to be highly competitive (Levich, 1978; Stockdale, 1978) the same must be supposed to be true of this sector of the loan market. Thirdly, Eurofinance markets are basically supply-orientated so that the participating institutions are systematically committed to finding outlets for funds except in occasional periods of severe uncertainty such as arose during 1974 and has occurred again in recent months. This last explanation appears to be the best founded of the three.

There is no clear evidence however to support any firm conclusion. It can be argued, quite correctly, that when the spreads and levels of interest rates charged to various countries are analyzed, these can be seen to drop where a country shows clear improvement in the balance of payments. The opposite influence can also be detected. In either case, this would suggest sovereign risk rather than liquidity influencing the market. As against that the spreads between countries have not varied greatly from one period to another with the exception of the two years from late 1974 to late 1976.

One argument frequently brought against the liquidity or supply-orientated theory of spread has been the variability in the US balance of payments in recent years. It is claimed that with the USA as the major reserve currency and its deficits thrusting funds upon Eurofinance markets, variability in supply should be reflected in shifts in spreads. But this has not been witnessed nor should we expect it, for US deficits offer no greater supply of funds than a similar deficit in any other country making payments abroad. In its 1971 Annual Report the West German Bundesbank, after dwelling upon capital flows from the USA, went on to say (1972, p. 36):

Money is created in the Euro-money market in particular, when central banks do not invest their dollar reserves in the United States itself but rather in the Euro-money market in order to obtain a higher interest rate. A similar effect comes about when, in a system with reserves held primarily in dollars, central banks switch their reserves out of the dollar into other currencies.

As explained in earlier chapters it is not the USA alone which generates the whole stock even of real dollars circulating in the Eurosystem, much less the stock of debt designated in US dollars. A narrow concentration on the USA's foreign economic position does not provide a basis for arguing against a supply orientated theory of spread.

Measurement of market performance and risk is complicated by the imposition of various fees and the possibility of some participating financial intermediaries not having to offer LIBOR schedules to attract deposits. In either case the esti-mate of spreads and potential earnings from loans is less certain. Of the two complications, variation in the way in which fees are imposed is the more likely to confuse the real significance of spreads. For example, spreads may not alter significantly while fees are increased or switched from payment over the term of the loan to a 'front-end' charge when the loan is established. Other techniques of lending adding to the diffi-culty of measurement are: the revolving credit line, a facility which allows a borrower flexibility during the life of a loan agreement in borrowing, repaying and borrowing again; grace periods before commencing repayment of principal; options to switch currencies of denomination, and variations in amort-ization provisions. Yet it must be recognized that many of the techniques devised in Eurofinance markets were introduced for the purposes of hedging risk.

Increased maturities associated with easing of the market are linked to maintaining profitability so long as the conven-tional relationship of rising yields with lengthening maturities holds. In this way, there is some offsetting to the reduced spreads over LIBOR. However, an easing market accelerates positive maturity transformation. Market circumstances create the basis for extending the liquidity position of borrowers. But this process increases risk for lenders; longer commitments increase the chances of unforseeable disturbances occurring. Furthermore, the shape of the yield curve determines the relative attractions of shifting to longer maturities.

(iv)   *General Features of Risk*

Unlike the position in international money markets, less scope exists for assessing the *pattern* of risk in the international bond market than with direct lending by participating financial intermediaries. Dealers in international bonds arrange placements between major holders rather than operating steadily in a more formal setting akin to national stock exchanges with many participants as buyers or sellers. The range of bonds traded by dealers, and changes in that range, go some way to reflect the risks attached to the bonds. Marketability is therefore closely tied to acceptable risk. In this respect the bond dealer provides an assessment of risk when distinguishing those bonds in which the dealer is active in making a market and those which will be traded on request of a buyer or seller.

But given the relative size of the various segments in Euro-finance markets, most attention attaches to risks with direct lending rather than bond issues. Thus the size of the spread between lending and borrowing determines the capacity to earn a return on funds sufficient to provide for a reserve fund against risk. An example may illustrate the basis of worries about narrowing of spreads. Supposing the capital/total assets ratio of a participating financial institution is 5 percent, with a company tax rate of 50 percent this intermediary must earn 20 percent on its capital to earn a 10 percent net profit. A gross return of 20 percent can be obtained when the spread is 1 percent given that the capital/total asset ratio is 5 percent. The question remains as to whether or not a net 10 percent return is a sufficient return on capital at the same time providing a margin for risk. One is tempted to doubt whether the capital/assets ratio is generally as much as 5 percent, especially as this would imply that the total capital of participating banks is of the order of \$125 billion.

The position would be further disguised if equity capital comprised a small proportion of total capital owing to past accumulations of reserves. However, an apparently satisfactory return on equity capital generated in this way would be an implicit admission of a declining willingness to accumulate · reserves. In that circumstance increased business might gradually erode the capital/asset ratio. The intermediary would be increasingly exposed to danger of failure should problems arise with loans.

Thus intermediaries may seek to offset the impact of narrow spreads by minimizing tax commitments so reducing the margin between gross and net return on capital. This tendency may be reflected in the amount of business formally organized through low tax economies in the Caribbean, amongst other places. In the more advanced financial centers, the real impact of tax is determined more by the administration of provisions when determining taxable income. Much depends on those tax provisions permitting the setting aside of margins for risk, or some similar implied cost, before determining that proportion of the gross return subject to tax.

On the other hand, in the light of the understandings between central banks and between central banks and the parent companies of participating financial intermediaries, the degree of risk to these intermediaries may be overstated. Since 1974 when the Herstatt and Franklin National problems arose, there have existed various arrangements for supporting a weakened participant. Most notable are the commitments exacted by the Bank of England from the participating institutions in London that they would be supported by their parent company or companies. This means that national monetary authorities are, one way or another, underwriting the risk exposure of the market. This exposure involves these authorities in borrowers' and lenders' commercial risk, sovereign risk and foreign exchange risk.

At the same time market participants have devised various means to minimize some risks. Short-term liquidity problems are anticipated by the extensive interbank market in deposits and loans as well as by negotiation of standby facilities such as lines of credit. Foreign currency contingencies are provided for in similar fashion. At least amongst the major banks and their subsidiaries, arrangements have been made for credit lines in foreign exchange as a mutual support when sharp fluctuations in rates and availability are experienced.

(v)   *Exchange Rates*

The actions of authorities and participating intermediaries during the past seven years illustrate the intimate links between Eurocurrency activities and foreign exchange transactions and rates. This has raised questions regarding the role of Eurobanks as a source of instability in foreign exchange markets. Some arguments for controlling directly the workings of Eurocurrency markets have been based upon the scope for foreign exchange speculation available in these markets. Very large sums regularly turned over in Eurofinance markets are readily available for currency redesignation, with substantial impact on relativities between currencies. There is no question about the role of Eurofinancing in extending markets for exchange transactions. Maturity transformation associated with the workings of the Eurofinance markets in general has increased the total supply of monies available. But the scale of foreign exchange transactions is not as greatly affected by this phenomenon as the flows of funds into the market, a significant share of which is contributed by central banks and similar authorities. During 1979 some US$37 billion of official foreign exchange reserves were placed in Eurofinance markets. Central bank deposits in these markets amounted to about $155 billion at the end of 1979. Moreover, it is admitted that in recent years some smaller central banks have engaged in shifting of funds (Wallich, 1979, p. 7):

it is the smaller central banks that may, and recently have, engaged in some switching from one currency to another, especially out of dollars.

Clearly, the alternative currency is the Deutschmark. The DM is also the main intervention currency when official action is taken to smooth dollar rate fluctuations.

Further, the size of the market affords opportunities for the private shifting of large sums from one currency to another as opposed to manipulations by the participating institutions (Mayer, 1976, p. 5):

> the facilities of the Eurocurrency banks can be used by large operators in the exchange market to mobilize large sums in a matter of minutes. The accusations that the banks themselves have engaged in collusive speculative maneuvers are not, however, supported by our data on changes in banks' net positions in specific foreign currencies.

The real issue is not so much the workings of the market but those circumstances generating the conditions in which speculative shifts against the dollar, or any other currency for that matter, might succeed. Critical in this matter is the state of domestic economic policy arrangements. Flows of funds between the USA and Eurofinance markets are symptomatic of difficulties rather than a cause of disturbance. Attitudes towards prospective exchange rate relativities reflect assessments of likely output, trade and price performances as well as interest rate possibilities. Policy measures within the USA or any major economy contributing to the funding of the Eurofinance market have their impact upon that market. Most attention, probably wrongly, does focus on the USA because of its role as holder of the major reserve currency. However, during late 1979 and much of 1980 there were many indications of a greater reliance upon the DM as a reserve currency. The need of the German authorities to finance their trade deficit by placing DM-denominated bonds with foreign central banks marked a further development towards a multi-currency reserve system. Different elements in policy merit examination. Those contributing to the exchange rate imbroglio mainly reflect short-term policy measures related to monetary and fiscal arrangements. Connections between domestic monetary and financial arrangements and international lending markets reflect longstanding institutional and policy practices.

(vi)   *Eurocurrencies and Market Behavior*

Exchange rate determinations in Eurocurrency markets embrace hedging operations in relation to borrowing and lending commitments by the participating institutions as well as by those providing, or having access to, funds. Had Eurofinance markets not existed in their present form, funds now flowing to that market would have been held somewhere by central banks and similar agencies as well as by commercial banks, firms and individuals. Unless a rigorous system of exchange controls had been implemented, speculative operations would still have occurred as holders sought to shift funds from a currency about which there were doubts on the stability of existing rates with other currencies. And, as experience with the postwar fixed exchange rate regime showed, even rigorous applications of control mechanisms often failed to prevent major exchange rate adjustments. The maturity transformation features of Eurofinance markets may have added to problems but this would be marginal to the effects arising from the dramatic rise in total funds available for shifting. Nevertheless the efficiency of Eurofinance markets must have increased the speed with which doubts about existing exchange rates have been communicated.

The foreign exchange functions of Eurofinance markets cannot help but influence exchange relativities. The total accumulations held in Eurofinance portfolios bear upon the supply and demand for different currencies and the determination of their prices. This is not to say that substantial changes in annual dollar outflows do not influence the foreign exchanges as well as the existing stock of debt, especially in regard to expectations. The highly liquid nature of the participating institutions' liabilities ensures that substantial funds can be mobilized for currency switching at any time doubts arise about existing relativities. Changes in rates can arise from the influx of one denomination or another to these markets or, more correctly, an anticipation of this taking place should existing rates be maintained.

The actions of participating institutions in matching spot and forward exchange commitments to secure covered positions for their forward transactions can bring in more funds. A partial explanation for the increase in direct lending by American banks during the latter part of 1978 is to be found in the workings of this segment of the market. At that time the heavy forward sales of dollars brought a large forward premium for strong currencies, such as the DM, so the Eurofinancing institutions sold dollars spot for those currencies to match forward commitments. Then, to finance those sales, they borrowed dollars in the USA. Yet the foreign exchange transactions associated with spot and forward markets would take place regardless of the existence of Eurofinancing markets in as much as covered arbitrage, taking into account interest differentials, is essential to international financing. That so much takes place through Eurofinance markets is merely a reflection of their technical efficiency. The emphasis on the dollar reflects the convenience of a central reserve currency and the size of the New York market compared with other financial centers.

The misconception that frequently occurs is to associate foreign exchange functions with the expansion of the Eurodollar loan market. Eurodebt would grow with the accumulation of funds from surplus countries funding deficits in other countries and for other reasons previously discussed. Further, the interest differentials favoring the Eurodollar market compared with national capital markets encourages funding in this way. But interventions by monetary authorities to stabilize currency adjustments can add to the markets through swap arrangements and various credit devices to support those currencies undergoing relative declines. It is this injection of new funds, in the sense of money created by central banks, which frequently adds to inflationary pressure. In short it is not speculation but the efforts to thwart exchange rate instability that generates additional money flows to the currency markets. The scale of these interventions has been substantial; in 1978 the gross value of interventions was US$50 billion as some fourteen central banks made concerted efforts to support currencies, mainly the US dollar, which were declining in foreign exchange markets (Deutsche Bundesbank, 1980, pp. 46–47).

(vii)   *Dollar—Deutschmark Exchanges*

There are important lessons to be learned from the recent experiences in foreign exchange markets with the gyrations of the US dollar rate since late 1979, following the shift in the strategy of monetary policy by the Federal Reserve Board on 6 October 1979. Up to that time most discussion and analysis had been directed to the problems of the dollar overhang represented by obligations in Eurofinancing markets and the holdings in foreign exchange reserves of various countries. Little attention had been given to the possibility of these markets working both ways, that is, to what might happen if the USA improved its trade position and domestic monetary and financial policies were adapted to international circumstances rather than designed to isolate the USA from external repercussions. The impact of change is clearly seen in what has taken place since October 1979.

Prior to October 1979 the dollar weakened as a result of the erosion of a restrictive monetary policy initiated in November 1978 but relaxed from April 1979. Between June and late September the Bundesbank in concert with the Federal Reserve acted to support the dollar. German support amounted to about DM18.6 billion in less than four months. When the Americans embarked on further restrictive policies some support was still needed, but following the announcement of the new monetary policy on 6 October 1979 the extent of official support was negligible for the remainder of the year. However there was some switching to dollars in the private sector. But early in 1980 the dollar firmed against other currencies and the Bundesbank moved to support the mark. While this action was not necessary after April 1980 further dollar sales were required between August and October. For the first ten months of the year the Bundesbank sold about US$10 billion of dollars to support the mark.

During this period there were other realignments of exchange rates as well as interventions particularly within the European Monetary System (EMS). But what is emerging is a dollar–Deutschmark axis where each responds to the ebb and flow of funds themselves reflecting interest rate differentials, expectations of inflation and balance of payments prospects. Increasingly the mark is performing a role as an intermediary currency for other European economies seeking access to funds. In part this appears to reflect a judgment that foreign exchange risk associated with the mark is not large given the arrangements in the EMS. But it may also reflect a judgment on relative stability compared with the gyrations of the dollar since late 1978. This spells out the reasons for the mark being more widely used as a reserve currency. It has become quite simply an appropriate vehicle for hedging risk in circumstances when the major reserve currency is prone to disturbance for whatever reason.

The problem for this shift towards a second reserve currency is the risk of large fluctuations in exchange rates and domestic interest rates when the mark's foreign exchange function is not supported by broad financial markets comparable to those available in the USA. Rapid switches in funds into and out of holdings in such circumstances may have exaggerated repercussions. In turn those domestic repercussions may risk a reinforcing of the very causes that had produced the initial disturbance. The Bundesbank is well aware of the potential risks of the enhanced role of its currency in international markets (1980, p. 56).

(viii)   *A Final Comment*

The position of the Eurofinance market in 1980 is not the same as it was in 1973 prior to the rapid escalation in real prices for crude oil and its derivatives. Since that year Eurobanks have accommodated many economies relying upon oil imports which experienced a marked worsening in their balance of payments. But the expansion in Eurofinancing, as we have so often observed above, served only to reduce pressures on these same deficit countries and others to adapt their policies and economic structures to a situation of easy borrowing. What this has meant is the accumulation of debt with international lenders so that the scope for further lending is limited by the risks of holding a high proportion of intermediaries' assets in a relatively few countries.

The risks associated with existing portfolios of assets held by participating financial intermediaries is compounded by the uncertainties in foreign exchange markets. These uncertainties are often associated with the relative size and growth of Eurofinance markets themselves, sometimes as a consequence of confusion between the accumulation of debt − the deposits − in Eurofinance markets and real money. But liquifying deposits is only possible by having access to dollars or the other currencies in which they are denominated, in the countries of the relevant currency. Thus any attempt to switch currencies or to shift out of Eurofinance markets is liable to generate rapid changes in exchange rates exacerbating the uncertainties that set off the movement in the first place.

What is believed to be the central issue is well (if possibly wrongly) attested, namely, that there is no substitute for a stable central reserve currency. This was clearly stated by the Bundesbank in its 1979 Annual Report (1980, p. 56):

> Pressures to diversify foreign exchange holdings will probably not ease until the United States durably succeeds in achieving better equilibrium in its balance of payments − the principal source of international liquidity in the past − and in stabilising

the dollar in the foreign exchange markets so as to make it sufficiently attractive for investible funds again.

Until this is achieved central banks, acting individually or in concert, will be required to pursue interventionist policies to smooth short-term gyrations in exchange rates. And neither stable currencies nor stable exchange rates will ever be achieved until there is a return to proper money and balanced international payments (see Chapter 7 below).

References

Aliber, R. Z. (1978), *Exchange Risk and Corporate International Finance* (New York: Halsted).

Andreas, K. (1979), 'Kapitalmarkt im Spannungsfeld von nationalen und internationalen Einflussen', Association of International Bond Dealers, Munchen, 4 Mai (Deutsche Bundesbank, Auszuge aus Presseartikeln, No. 31, 9 Mai).

Deutsche Bundesbank (1972), *Report for the Year 1971*, 12 April.

Deutsche Bundesbank (1980), *Report for the Year 1979*, April.

Levich, R. M. (1978), 'Tests of forecasting models and market efficiency in the international money market', in J. A. Frenkel and H. G. Johnson (eds), *The Economics of Exchange Rates* (Reading, Mass.: Addison-Wesley), Ch. 8, pp. 129–58.

McKinnon, R. I. (1977), *The Eurocurrency Market*, Essays in International Finance, No. 125, December (Princeton: International Finance Section, Princeton University), p. 40.

Mayer, H. W. (1976), 'The BIS concept of the Eurocurrency market', *Euromoney*, May, pp. 60–6.

Solomon, A. M. (1979a), *Statement*, Joint Hearing of Sub-Committees of the Committee on Banking, Finance and Urban Affairs, US House of Representatives, 12 July.

Solomon, A. M. (1979b), Attachment to the *Statement*: 'The financing of payments imbalances and activity in international capital markets'.

Stockdale, A. C. (1978), 'Risk, information and forward exchange rates', in J. A. Frenkel and H. G. Johnson (eds), *The Economics of Exchange Rates* (Reading, Mass.: Addison-Wesley), pp. 159–78.

Wallich, H. (1979), 'Euro-Markets and U.S. monetary growth', *Journal of Commerce*, May 1 and 2, transcript version.

Wallich, H. (1978), 'International lending and the Euro-markets', Euro-markets Conference sponsored by the *Financial Times*, London, 9 May 1978.

6 Some Euromarket Folklore

(i) *An Official View*

In this chapter we look at and comment upon certain official pronouncements and proposals on the subject of Eurofinance which give an insight into the beliefs and doubts of those who operate, or who might have some responsibility for overseeing, the system as a whole.

As long as Eurobanks are thought of as banks and not as moneylenders it is natural to associate their activities with money creation and, accordingly, to be concerned about 'control'. National governments do not cede lightly to international institutions, economic powers which might bear upon domestic employment or the domestic price level. Fears have been expressed also that the ready availability of Eurofinance for both domestic and foreign investment might undermine home fiscal as well as monetary policies.

There is an ever present contradiction. On the one hand it appears necessary, from time to time, to offer internationally coordinated support to the Eurocurrency system to sustain the flow of trade or to inhibit exaggerated movements in exchange rates. On the other hand it is impossible to be entirely unaware of the extent to which the mere existence of Eurobanks, so supported, restricts the economic options previously thought to be open to national governments. The twentieth century is coming to understand once again what the nineteenth century knew so well. No one can eat his cake and have it too.

Sentiments such as this no doubt underlie US and other efforts to introduce legislation laying down rules of conduct for the Euromarket intended, hopefully, to secure the best of all worlds for everyone. One such set of proposals was embodied in a US Bill entitled, 'Euro-currency Control Act of 1979, H.R. 3962', aimed at imposing reserve requirements on participating institutions in much the same way as now applies to member banks of the Federal Reserve System. To be successful the measure would require the cooperation of other countries. Discussions of this proposal before subcommittees of the House of Representatives reflect US thinking on problems of, and measures to deal with, the situation as it was understood at the time.

The Hon. A. M. Solomon, the Under Secretary of the Treasury for Monetary Affairs, summarized the issues as follows (Solomon, 1979, p. 3):

> the size of the Eurocurrency market and the rate of its growth have led to expressions of concern and to fears that:
> - the Eurocurrency market was itself generating or creating excessive amounts of credits;
> - banks were incurring excessive risks;
> - the ready availability of such large sources of credit contributed to destabilizing speculation on the foreign exchange markets,
> - and more recently, that the Eurocurrency market was complicating efforts to appraise and manage domestic monetary conditions.

It is possible to share some of the anxieties expressed in these comments yet at the same time to wonder whether the US Treasury is (or was) entirely clear as to the precise nature of the problem. As we have so often explained in earlier chapters, the Euromarket has no power to *create* 'credit' of any kind. It cannot lend one single dollar more than is deposited with it. Only banks with checking systems can lend what they have not got; and to be a checking bank it is necessary to be part of a bank clearing system. Although the next step in the future might actually be to develop a check clearing system, or its equivalent, for checks drawn on Eurobanks, there is no evidence that anything of this kind yet exists. US dollars can be created *only* by the US banking system. All that Eurobanks can do is to give confidence in their lending activities to persons or banks who *already have* dollars. The same applies to all other countries.

In these circumstances it is hard to see why the US Treasury expresses its fears in the terms it does. The 'excessive creation of credit' can only mean the excessive encouragement of international lending. The danger lies in the unconstrained growth of that debt and the consequent destruction of the trade balancing mechanism not in the (improperly supposed) 'fact' that dollars (?credits) are being brought into being outside of the USA. This last is simply not true. Even where swap agreements create new dollars which find their way into Eurobanks the damage is done, not by Eurobanks, but by the central bank or clearing banks of the country whose money is being 'printed'.

Nor, in the remarks quoted, is the precise nature of the 'excessive risk' made plain. On the face of it, when A lends to B the only risk is borne by A, who might not get his money back. If a Eurobank underwrites the risk then it assumes part of the risk, but this in no way commands the involvement of authorities in the country in whose currency the debt is designated. Of course it is true that US citizens might be implicated, as individuals in the transaction, if, that is, either A or B or a member of the board of the Eurodollar bank happens to be a US national. But even then the risk is no business of the US government or its Federal Reserve System unless the one or the other chooses to make it its business. If a bank makes risky loans and in consequence fails why should any government or central bank feel impelled to come to its aid at the expense of the rest of the community, given that inflation must follow? Not only is this unfair but it removes the necessity for the very function the bank is paid to perform, that is, to carry the risk. If governments do come to the aid of private banks then they have only themselves to blame. At the same time they should recognize that, by the fact of coming to the rescue, they are undermining the value of the very currency they are trying to protect.

It is true, of course, and we have made much of this, that the existence of a huge international short-term debt can have, and in present circumstances does have, a destabilizing effect on exchange rates. But this is not a necessary consequence of debt *per se*. It is a consequence of the way the debt is handled. If international debt were not short term to lenders and if lenders did not enjoy the right to redesignate the currency at will, and if Eurobanks were much less involved than they are in currency transactions, as opposed to borrowing and lending, the destabilizing effect of debt might be much less.

Finally it seems worth pointing out once again that the ease with which a domestic currency might be borrowed abroad is not simply the direct consequence of the existence of Eurobanks. No more and no less money can be borrowed from abroad (whether Eurobanks exist or not) than has been created by banks in the home country. Furthermore money which has been borrowed from abroad must, even before it was borrowed, already have existed as a foreign owned deposit in a bank *within* the borrowing country. In other words, it is not possible to borrow from abroad *one's own* currency without first having created foreign held deposits at home with *one's own* excessive imports. And in turn excessive imports are more often than not created by excessive money creation at home. Governments which identify the Eurodollar market as the cause of their badly managed domestic monetary affairs would find, if they looked deeper, that it is their own badly managed domestic monetary affairs that confer upon the Eurodollar market the very power to 'interfere' about which they are complaining.

All of this is not intended to show that the existence of the Eurodollar market is not a cause for concern. What it does show, however, is that wrongly identified causes for concern lead to incorrect proposals for reform. The imposition of reserve requirements upon Eurobanks might very well raise rates of interest and indeed may have the effect of diminishing the amount of international lending channeled through the Euromarket. But it could have no effect upon the growth of international debt itself unless at the same time it managed, by some thus far unspecified mechanism, to correct current imbalances of trade or payments.

Those in favor of Eurobank reserve requirements would of

course be on stronger ground if their objectives were less concerned with the wider problems of inflation, the money supply and of international trade and more with the simpler question of avoiding the diversion of banking business from the USA to Europe. Some of this at least must have been in the mind of Representative J. Leach, sponsor of the Bill mentioned previously, who argued in testimony before sub-committees of the House of Representatives (Leach, 1979, p. 11):

> Reserve requirements of Eurocurrency deposits should have the effect of: (1) raising the cost of funds in the Eurocurrency market, thereby removing the competitive advantage this market offers international institutions vis-à-vis the domestic market; and (2) putting a limit on the amount of credit which can be created in the Eurocurrency market. As a result, it would be less advantageous for financial institutions to make extensive use of Eurocurrencies for both their lending and foreign exchange operations, as well as to circumvent domestic monetary controls. The Bill therefore seeks to improve the conduct of monetary policy, help control inflation and make disruptive currency speculation more difficult.

Even so Representative Leach continues to speak of the 'creation of credit' rather than the onlending of funds and the 'circumvention of domestic monetary controls' rather than discriminatory rules governing US bank portfolios as opposed to banks abroad.

Other approaches to the regulation of Eurofinance markets have been pursued elsewhere. For the most part these discussions have been conducted under the auspices of the Bank for International Settlements (BIS, 1979, 1980, pp. 113–15). Attention has been devoted to the general impact of international lending on world economic conditions, the supposed reduced capacities of national monetary authorities to conduct their policies and to questions relating to the stability of the participating financial institutions. There is little agreement on the likely macroeconomic impacts of the Euromarket though there is a ubiquitous claim (probably false) that, by increasing the velocity of circulation of national monetary aggregates and by providing a means for central banks readily to shift currencies in which foreign exchange reserves are held, Eurofinance markets may exacerbate world problems of inflation.

Where there is more agreement is in the matter of supervision of the behavior of participating institutions when conducting international lending: The Deutsche Bundesbank (1980, p. 49), as an important contributor to these discussions, recognizes in particular the implications for the whole financial structure should there be difficulties with one or a few participating institutions.

All these worries over control and supervision are reviewed in subsequent sections. First, the American position is examined in greater detail. This is followed by a study of the 'European' position as exemplified by the work of the BIS.

(ii) *Domestic Monetary Management*

The fear that Eurofinance markets obstruct domestic monetary management particularly affects those economies whose currencies are widely held internationally; hence the long-standing concern on this matter of the legislative and administrative branches of government in the USA.

According to Henry Wallich (1979, p. 8):

> While the Eurocurrency market is linked to domestic markets and subject to control through the impact of domestic monetary policy on interest rates, it does pose problems for monetary policy. My judgement is that these problems have been of only moderate significance to date, but they are increasing. Moreover, the Eurocurrency market adds to inflationary pressures because liabilities to nonbanks in this market are rising faster than domestic money supplies. In the present inflationary environment we must look closely at every source of inflationary pressure.

As with many semi-public pronouncements it is not easy here

to follow the train of thought. Nor is the full text of much help. We know of course that growth in Euromarket liabilities to non-banks in no way measures the growth in the world stock of real dollars, for it simply records the change in the cumulative total of non-bank lending through Eurobanks. If every person in the world (including US citizens) who held dollar deposits in current accounts in US banks transferred those deposits to Eurobanks there would be an enormous growth in Eurobank liabilities to non-banks but no growth at all in the world stock of dollars. Nor would there be any change in the total of deposits in US banks. All that would be observed would be a change of ownership of deposits in the USA from non-bank holders (home and foreign) to Eurobanks. And if the Eurobanks onlent their newly acquired dollars to precisely the same persons who had deposited them the only change observed would be an enormous and permanent increase in the ratio of non-bank deposits in Eurobanks to the world stock of dollars. Spending could go on just as before. And since the world stock of dollars would be unchanged it would be illogical to suppose any 'addition to inflationary pressures'. What therefore can the quoted statement mean?

The probability would seem to be that Mr Wallich believed, at the time of giving evidence, that all Eurodollar deposits were truly money and that he specified 'non-bank deposits' only because he wished to avoid double counting. If this were the case he must have been supposing that a proportionate increase in Eurodeposits greater than the proportionate increase in the domestic money stock would somehow reflect the creation of new dollars outside the USA thereby generating a potential threat to the stability of prices inside the USA. But as we have shown so many times above this is a totally wrong view.

If this wrong view were accepted, however, it would naturally provoke an interest in the proportion of the supposed newly created dollars likely to be spent in the USA. Conversely there would be, as indeed there is, an interest in the growth in the stock of real dollars needed as international currency reserves and in whether dollar currency reserves were being supplanted by other currencies, especially the Deutschmark (Deutsche Bundesbank, 1979, p. 50). But of course all such enquiries would, in this context, be misguided. As long as no one is creating new money the onlending of funds through Eurobanks will not of itself be inflationary. With some easily identified exceptions (see, for example, McKinnon, 1977) there can be no flow of funds into the Euromarket without a trade surplus somewhere which means in turn that somewhere in the world there must exist goods for the borrowers of Euro-funds to buy. (See Chapter 2 above.) Naturally if borrowers seek to buy goods other than those available this will lead to price rises in some goods. But this kind of price rise should be welcomed and recognized, not as inflation, but as part of the adjustment process which clears markets and, except in the circumstances outlined in Chapter 2 above, balances trade.

A more real issue is that referred to above, namely, the question of the diversion of bank business from the USA to Europe to escape home-financial controls. This is a matter of institutional arrangements and policy techniques of which the former seem the more significant at present. Most prominent is the imposition of reserve requirements on member banks of the Federal Reserve System. This device, based upon the traditional banking concept of maintaining some proportion of commercial bank assets in liquid form, imposes a cost on member banks. Thus, by comparison with the income-earning potential of other financial intermediaries to which reserve requirements do not apply, member banks must seek higher returns from the remainder of their asset portfolios if earnings ratios are to be competitive with other firms in the capital market. Membership may offer possibilities of attracting liabilities at lower cost but, given deposit insurance arrangements, this is a doubtful point, at best.

There is an incentive for those commercial banks, being members of the Federal Reserve System, to seek higher returns from foreign lending in order to compensate for the domestic impost arising from reserve requirements. This trend has been reinforced by the relatively declining share of the larger banks in the total banking activity of the USA (Wallich, 1978, p. 9). But the attractions of possible higher earnings abroad are not confined to major member banks. Restraints on some interest rates, and a ban on interest payments on short-term deposits of less than thirty days, encourage companies with deposit balances to shift into money markets with possibilities for greater earnings. Eurofinancing institutions, often the affiliates or subsidiaries of American banks, can offer these opportunities because they do not have to meet the cost of holding non-income-earning assets in the USA. There is an institutional bias in present American banking provisions encouraging shifts to Eurofinancing whether for assets or liabilities. As noted above, this competitive handicap to major banks was well recognized by the congressional sponsor of US proposals for controlling Eurocurrency markets, see quotation above on page 110.

These circumstances help to explain why, despite the emphasis to the contrary in this book, the rate of growth in deposits with Eurofinancing institutions is not dependent *solely* upon balance of payments deficits and surpluses as measured in conventional terms, that is, on current account or that measure plus direct foreign investment. There are relative attractions in placing funds in Eurofinancing institutions rather than national capital markets regardless of the trade payments position. These aspects are quite separate from the actions of central banks shifting funds into or out of Eurofinance markets.

The cause for Euromarket growth set out in the previous paragraph is not however a property of the Euromarket as such. A similar explanation is to be found for the steady decline in the proportion of US domestic banks who are members of the Federal Reserve System. Further, the non-bank financial intermediaries not facing reserve requirements, such as money market mutual funds, are able to attract business in the same way by offering income-earning opportunities not matched by commercial banks. Declining bank membership of the Federal

Reserve System also undermines the capacity to establish desired monetary policies, given that those policies are what they are. This was clearly spelt out by the then Chairman of the Board of Governors of the Federal Reserve System, Mr G. William Miller, in testimony to the Committee on Banking, Housing and Urban Affairs (Miller, 1979, p. 2):

> As a larger fraction of the deposits at banks becomes subject to the diverse reserve requirements set by the 50 states rather than by the Federal Reserve, and as more transactions balances reside at thrift institutions, the relationship between the money supply and reserves controlled by the Federal Reserve will become less and less predictable, and the instruments of monetary policy will become less precise in their application.

Since 1970 Federal Reserve member banks' share of total commercial banks' deposits has fallen from about 81 per cent to 72 per cent. This downward drift is claimed to have increased the unpredictability of short-term estimates of the growth of monetary aggregates by about 50 per cent (Federal Reserve Board Staff, 1979, Chart 1). However, this official interpretation must be based upon some belief in a direct proportionate link between member banks' share and unpredictability. This argument is not convincing because it ignores the liquidity needs of non-member banks. None the less, the constant recurrence of expressions of doubt on the capacity to achieve effective monetary management in the face of recent trends cannot be ignored. Hence, even if the point were taken, the workings of Eurofinance markets cannot be blamed exclusively for shortcomings in monetary performance. Indeed the very institutional arrangement encouraging participation in Eurofinancing might itself be blamed for some part of the flight from membership of the Federal Reserve System.

(iii)   *US Reserve Requirements Proposals*

Details of the US proposals are as follows. Reserve requirements would be set on a basis comparable to those applying to member banks of the Federal Reserve System. In recognition of the interdependency of interests amongst national governments permitting substantial Eurocurrency dealings within their borders, the measure would only be implemented when agreement was reached on the reserve ratios to be applied amongst countries having 75 per cent of the total business. The important question of measuring that activity, difficult as it has been for the BIS, is not faced.

The aim of the proposal is twofold: to make Federal Reserve member banks competitive with the participating institutions in the Eurocurrency market and to bring that market under the direct policy jurisdiction of national monetary authorities. The proposals presume that each national government has the power to reach all the subsidiaries and affiliates associated with the financial institutions registered within its borders. The authorities are to extend their claims to sovereignty, and hence supervision, of activities in branches and the like wherever they are domiciled. Other governments may not accept the same role, or subscribe to the same notions of sovereignty, as those advanced by the USA. Cooperation therefore may prove less easy than is assumed in the proposal.

This aspect aside, other complications should be spelt out. The means of operating the scheme are not clear in view of the interests of host governments. Some of the issues have been listed in documents supporting official testimony (Federal Reserve Board Staff, 1979). But central to the discussion is the method of determining the application and supervision of reserve requirements and the ways in which reserve deposits might be held by monetary authorities in participating countries.

Reserve requirements could be imposed in a variety of ways: first, by the central bank in the country to which the head office of the banking network belongs; secondly, by the central bank in the host country in which the activities take place; and, thirdly, by the central bank in which the currencies of the Eurofinancing markets are denominated. Added complications would arise with consortium banks having partners from different countries of origin. The first and third approaches would place a substantial part of the responsibility with the Federal Reserve Board while control under the second arrangement would be much more widely dispersed. The first scheme is tantamount to seeking the cooperation of the monetary authorities in other countries to supervise their branches, subsidiaries and affiliates in the same way as the American authorities now oversee their own domestic and foreign activity.

Yet the method chosen cannot be independent of the ways in which the reserves are to be held. Under the first and third schemes the American authorities would stand to gain from earnings on the reserves accruing to them as the funds were placed in government bonds or notes. Hence, it is argued, some device would have to be found for distributing those earnings amongst the participating central banks or governments. Otherwise the host governments might believe themselves to be losing tax and employment possibilities with the imposition of reserve requirements, especially in that part of the avowed purpose of the scheme is to reverse the competitive handicaps to the American banking system, or at least to the member banks in the Federal Reserve System. Should the regulation not achieve this aim the whole venture would be fruitless. If the main intent were simply to preserve the liquidity of participating financial institutions then there are other ways of achieving this objective.

Placing reserves in the central bank or in government paper issued by the country in which the liabilities are denominated, while under the supervision of the central bank of the home country, is unlikely to be acceptable. More feasible might be a system of control and supervision by the central bank in the host country so that the earnings would arise and economic benefits accrue in the existing location of the market. Attempts at more complicated arrangements would be fraught with difficulty. They would require the creation of extensive exchange controls to halt leakages from the participating area of supervision, a feature well recognized in official commentaries (Federal Reserve Board Staff, 1979, pp. 9–10).

Reserve requirements would have to be common to all the participating central banks. Otherwise some centers would be at an advantage vis-à-vis expansion at the expense of others. It is conceivable that some countries would wish to exploit this advantage, if it existed, but only those whose currencies were prominent in the Eurocurrency market.

Another possibility would be for a uniform reserve requirement to be imposed for all countries with the proviso that even higher requirements might be applied by individual countries. In this way those countries wishing to restrain national institutions and their foreign subsidiaries and affiliates from engaging in Eurofinancing activities might be able to discourage participation. Such a step might have attractions for a government or central bank not wishing its currency to be used as a reserve currency. Yet this possibility would not stop Eurofinancing institutions accepting deposits and making loans denominated in the currency of that country. Both the German and Swiss experiences in recent years show how difficult it is to halt the use of a currency for reserve purposes, whatever the national monetary authorities may judge their interests to be in the matter.

Given that control is desired, what level of reserve requirement ought to be applied? Where the aim is to compensate for the existing lack of competitiveness of Federal Reserve member banks, the setting of reserve requirements would have to be harmonized with those applicable in the USA. Yet current American thinking reveals little agreement even over the home level and need for reserve requirements given the variety of types of deposits now carried. The greatest interest focuses of course upon the reserve requirement for transactions (i.e. current) deposits. In the testimony by the then Chairman of the Federal Reserve Board, referred to on page 115, appropriate reserve requirements were quoted according to various proposals before the Senate and the House as well as

Table 6.1 *Proposals for Reserve Requirements*

Deposit Category	Senate (S. Bill 85) Range	Senate (S. Bill 85) Initial	House of Representatives (H.R. Bill 7) Range	House of Representatives (H.R. Bill 7) Initial	Federal Reserve Board Range	Federal Reserve Board Initial
Transactions deposits	12–14	13	8–10	9.5	8–10	9.5
Short-term time	4–8	6	3–9	8	3–8	8
Savings	1–5	3	1–3	3	1–3	3
Long-term time	0.5–2	1	1–3	1	1–3	1

Source: Miller (1979).

suggestions from the Board. These are summarized in Table 6.1. Whatever the proposal, transactions deposits call for the highest reserves.

While these alternatives were presented as part of a debate on the domestic banking situation, they are indicative of the kind of structure which it is thought that Eurocurrency dealers might have to face. Suggestions for the scheme actually to be applied to Eurocurrency markets provide for a range of 2 to 5 percent on the following grounds (Federal Reserve Board Staff, 1979, p. 13):

> If the reserve requirement were set much above this level it might have an undesired impact on the profitability of Euro-currency banking and encourage large immediate shifts of funds to other Euro-markets, including Euro-security markets and offices of banks of nonparticipating countries located out-side participating countries, as well as shifts to national bank-ing systems. If the reserve requirement were set below this level it would be virtually meaningless.

However, there is a remarkable footnote to the first sentence in this quotation set against the word profitability. It reads,

Unless a market rate of interest were paid on the reserves held
at central banks. It is not at all clear that all central banks have
the authority to do so. Moreover, payment of a market rate on
Euro-currency reserves, but not on domestic reserves, would
tend to offset the restraining effect on Euro-markets of any
reserve requirement.

This quotation and its footnote go to the nub of the debate.
The problems of the American banking system, both in
relation to Eurofinancing and the decline of membership in the
Federal Reserve System, could be resolved at once within the
domestic institutional arrangements simply by offering
interest payments on the presently sterile reserve deposits.
Even if it were considered desirable to compensate the US bank
system in the manner proposed for the damage caused by its
own regulation, the plain truth is that the suggestion of a
2–5 percent range for reserve requirements in the Eurocurrency markets begs the question of the differing maturities
of deposits in Eurobanks and of course the almost complete
absence of transactions deposits in the ordinary banking sense.

(iv)　*A Challenge to National Sovereignty*

Two elements in the American proposals for inaugurating
reserve requirements merit close scrutiny. They are the
conception of sovereignty and the implicit exclusiveness of the
US dollar. Each may be challenged in different ways.

The conception of sovereignty confers on the supervising
authority in the country of origin explicit, if not dominant,
rights to review and change the basis on which business is
conducted by a branch, affiliate or subsidiary. Yet countries
other than USA are less certain of their reach beyond national
boundaries, especially where subsidiaries and affiliates are
incorporated as separate legal entities. Indeed efforts to restore
the relative competitiveness of the American banking system
at the cost of other economies, by imposing constraints upon
the workings of the whole of the international capital market
and by introducing a particular interpretation of sovereignty,

clearly invites retaliation. It raises the possibility of giving legislative status to 'arm's length' relationships between overseas branches, subsidiaries and affiliates and the monetary authorities in home countries as well as the head offices of participating institutions. Thus the official American position will inevitably be challenged. Such a challenge might well be ineffective were the US dollar unassailably the pre-eminent currency for international transactions that it used to be. But this pre-eminence, characterizing the two decades following the end of the Second World War, has been whittled away. Other currencies have come increasingly to the fore in trade and capital transactions. The leverage enjoyed by the US dollar has been significantly eroded. Similarly, the skills developed in a few financial centers have become much more diffused throughout the international community. Moreover this process has been accompanied by a capacity to develop new financial instruments appropriate to the time and setting.

So long as substantial real dollar balances (i.e. sight deposits in the USA) are held by non-residents and Eurobanks the US authorities are not in a position to dictate their use. Efforts to restrain the development of new centers and alternative uses of these balances risk the acceptability of the US dollar as a numeraire in international transactions. This project might further stimulate speculation against that currency, an outcome having the opposite effect to that sought by the proponents of reserve requirements. Reserve requirements restrict the use and hence the earnings of foreign held real dollars.

The US proposal pays little attention to substitution possibilities in the international capital market. This could come in two guises: the development of new international financial centers and the availability of alternative instruments other than bank loans.

The supposed and hoped for effectiveness of legislative cooperation with countries now controlling 75 percent of existing business rests upon expectations regarding the degree of control which can be secured on banking companies now participating in the markets and upon the assumption that major new banking and finance groups to handle the diversion of business will not develop. But the lesson of the rapid growth in Eurofinancing activities over this past decade is that new firms can and do develop. Moreover, new partnerships could emerge combining major existing firms and new enterprises in centers outside the reach of countries participating in the supervisory agreement. Facilities for transacting Eurofinancing business have grown in the Middle East, Asia and the Pacific. It would be foolhardy to claim that advantage would not be taken of any measures to restrain growth in the present major centers bordering the Atlantic.

Nor should the likelihood of the development of alternative techniques be ignored. The Eurocurrency market is the major but not the only component in Eurofinancing. Existing firms, especially the merchant banks, in British terminology, could shift their activities towards management and agency rather than deposit and lending functions. They could encourage the development of firms in new locations by acting as agents while supervising asset management on behalf of depositing clients. The managing agency has many historical precedents in trade and finance so that its application in this sphere would not be novel. Activities could also be developed in what is already a substantial market for commercial paper while negotiating foreign exchange and hedging through third parties in non-participating centers.

Most important, the Eurobond market already exists and stands alongside the Eurocurrency market with all the potentiality for switching into denominations and maturities now available in the deposit and lending markets. Closure of the loan market might simply give a stimulus to bond issues, strengthening that market by providing an even greater range of maturities and qualities of paper than is offered at present.

Another matter, separate from the preceding two, is the applicability of reserve requirements to those countries which do not now use that monetary instrument for the control of their banking systems. The US proposal raises questions touching on the feasibility of using simultaneously, yet in coordinated fashion, more than one instrument for monetary control. This calls for much more than mere agreement on the desired policies for national and international markets. Some countries may have chosen not to rely upon reserve requirement techniques for monetary control precisely because these are quantitative constraints not suited to internationally-oriented economies heavily dependent upon trade in goods and services.

It is sometimes argued that the burden of a non-income-earning asset requirement on a banking system can be exaggerated and that it is wrong to think that reserve requirements significantly impede the successful conduct of policy. But if this is so, why does the USA use this argument in its appeal for legislation? Indeed it is the burden itself which determines the impact of the policy. The regulation of banking can have discriminatory effects, akin to a tax, on equity holders, on banks, or their depositors or both (Johnson, 1972; Penner and Silber, 1973). These discriminatory features work by favoring the growth of financial institutions other than banks (a fact well documented in recent decades), stimulating the acquisition of assets having a higher risk exposure and a higher return. In some cases where portfolios are adjusted by shifting to liabilities or assets in alternative currencies, exchange rates themselves can be affected.

In all circumstances the failure to gain acceptance of the reserve requirement proposal is hardly surprising. National monetary authorities employ different techniques in their conduct of policy. The American proposal seeks to relieve problems inherent in its own domestic monetary management by imposing the same problems on everyone else.

(v)   *The Euromarket and Lenders of Last Resort*

The primary purpose of reserve requirements in a national banking system is to ensure that a minimum proportion of assets is deposited with the central bank. Initially this simply represented formalization of the traditional cash reserve necessarily held by any prudent bank. However, now seen as a monetary technique, the reserve has come to be thought of as a device influencing the capacity of banks to create money. Failure to maintain the required ratio implies borrowing from the central bank, often at penal rates, until such times as other assets can be made liquid. Thus a prudential arrangement geared to the potential demands of depositors, the holders of liabilities of a bank, became a regulatory technique affecting the asset structure of banks.

This monetary technique has to be supported by access to 'lender of last resort' facilities at the central bank. In what respect can this apply to participating financial institutions in Eurocurrency markets when dealing in currencies other than those of the country in which they are domiciled?

This question is crucial to any proposal seeking to regulate Eurocurrency markets. Access to central bank support might very well mean the injection of additional funds to the market almost upon demand. Yet since the Smithsonian Agreement of December 1971, there has been an understanding amongst the central banks of the so-called G-10 countries, comprising Belgium–Luxembourg, Canada, France, Germany, Italy, Japan, Netherlands, Sweden, the UK and the USA, to restrict their activities in all Eurofinance markets because of the stimulus it imparts. Switzerland also joined in this understanding (Deutsche Bundesbank, 1972, p. 54). Thus there are contradictions implicit in the very idea of imposing reserve requirements. Central bank support would add to funds available at precisely the moment when restraint was most desired. The very same contradictions emerge whenever central banks intervene, by one means or another, to stabilize exchange rate fluctuations. For example, in 1978 concerted intervention by fourteen central banks from the eleven countries mentioned above, plus those in Austria, Denmark and Ireland, placed a gross amount of US$50 billion in the Euromarket through purchases of dollars, though this was reduced to a net contribution less than half this sum by the end of the year (Deutsche Bundesbank, 1979, pp. 46–7).

In fact the wish to introduce reserve requirements into Euromarkets reflects an incorrect belief that what is being dealt with is comparable to a national banking system. It is not sufficiently understood that Eurofinancing activities are analogous only to non-bank financial intermediation. Fixed-term deposits are not the same as current deposits. Deposits with Eurofinancing institutions are not the same as current deposits with banks. To treat Eurofinancing institutions as if they were banks would be a serious mistake as long as Eurobanks cannot write checks on themselves but only on national banks with which they hold accounts. In this context debt is not money.

Any effort to introduce reserve requirements might very well result in the monetizing of the debts of Eurofinancing institutions by giving them direct access to central banks. A clearing system for Eurobanks might then develop and even more disastrous money printing begin.

(vi) *The European Approach*

This possibility might help to explain some of the disagreement on appropriate measures for supervising Eurofinance markets. Unlike the Americans, the European central banks have devoted attention to more direct supervisory methods of control. This approach emphasizes information, inspection and supervision of the structure of assets. Agreement on the first two aspects was reached amongst central banks of the G-10 group plus Switzerland in April 1979 (Deutsche Bundesbank, 1980, pp. 49–50; BIS, 1980, pp. 114–17). Some authorities, such as the Swiss, have carried this further with tighter rules on the proportion of loans to be placed in any one country as well as specified ratios of capital to assets. But the effectiveness of any such specification depends upon the consolidation of accounts for subsidiaries and affiliates.

The purposes to be served by this kind of supervision are straightforward. First, there is emphasis upon the need for information on what is taking place. Despite the very significant efforts by the BIS and the data collections of Morgan Guaranty, only the London segment of these markets is reasonably well recorded. Secondly, what is demanded is supervision of asset structures as a whole with special reference to risk.

The European view clearly reflects a different interpretation of the role of Eurocurrency markets than that underlying the American approach. Both the Germans and the Swiss emphasize the external stimulus to the growth of Eurofinancing from central bank deposits in participating institutions and the need for monetary and fiscal policies that will contain and then reduce balance of payments deficits. The general position was stated during 1978 in succinct terms (Leutwiler, 1978, p. 11):

> In the recent past, a tendency has emerged to push the solution of economic and foreign exchange policy problems from the national scene – where they appear to be unsolvable – on to the international arena. Salvation was often expected of summit meetings or of other international conferences. This has been true above all of international monetary arrangements; unfortunately experiences have been particularly disappointing.
>
> Certainly, international cooperation is indispensable in monetary and currency matters, and the present situation is – to put it mildly – capable of improvement. The success of such efforts, however, stands or falls in direct relation to how well certain norms of behavior are observed.

The central importance of national economic performance has been the persistent theme of the Deutsche Bundesbank in successive annual reports and statements throughout the 1970s. Although there is clear recognition of the need for cooperation between central banks for the efficient working of Eurofinance markets and effective supervision of those markets, the real problem is seen to lie with the policy conduct of national authorities with respect to inflation, the balance of payments and the switching of foreign exchange reserves. This position is summarized (Deutsche Bundesbank, 1979, pp. 52–3):

> The expansion of the international financial markets could more easily be kept within limits that are acceptable in terms of external monetary policy if the major countries were to agree jointly on a framework of conditions for these markets. This would of course be no substitute for stability-oriented fiscal and above all monetary policies in these countries. Given the continuing predominant role of the U.S. dollar as a financing and reserve currency and the sizable deficits on the U.S. current and capital accounts, the United States bears a particular responsibility in this connection.

It is encouraging to note in this quotation a proper emphasis upon the need for each country separately to set its house in order together with equally proper expressions of concern over risk. But even so it is difficult to escape the general conclusion that all published proposals, whatever their source, reflect some degree of misunderstanding as well as an uncomfortable mixture of private and/or national self-seeking combined with a deep-seated feeling of danger that something, we are not too sure what, might be going wrong. There remains, even in the Deutsche Bundesbank report, clear expressions of confidence that 'control' of the market is all that is needed and no recognition at all of the part played by the Eurodollar market in its own existence and growth. It is nowhere explained that inflation breeds debt, that debt generates a need for banking services and that as soon as there is a need for banking services banks appear. When inflation ends and debt declines, as one day it must, so too will banks. This is not only a matter of logic, it is the lesson of history. The Eurodollar market is an excrescence which like the Mississippi Bubble cannot survive. What is important is not that it should be guided along an orderly growth path to an adult life but that its immediate death should be engineered with a maximum of speed and a minimum of fuss. In our final chapter we considered both prognosis and prescription.

References

Bank for International Settlements (1979), *Forty-Ninth Annual Report 1978–1979*. Basle, 11 June.

Bank for International Settlements (1980), *Fiftieth Annual Report 1979–80*, Basle, 9 June.

Deutsche Bundesbank (1972), *Report for the Year 1971*, 12 April.

Deutsche Bundesbank (1979), *Report for the Year 1978*, 12 April.

Deutsche Bundesbank (1980), *Report for the Year 1979*, 17 April.

Federal Reserve Board Staff (1979), A Discussion Paper Concerning Reserve Requirements on Eurocurrency Deposits, 25 April (attachment to Henry Wallich, *Statement*, 12 July 1979; see Wallich, 1979, below).

Johnson, H. G. (1972), 'Problems of efficiency in monetary management', in H. G. Johnson (ed.), *Further Essays in Monetary Economics* (London: Allen & Unwin, pp. 88–112.

Leach, J. (1979), *Statement*, Joint Hearing of Sub-Committees of the Committee on Banking, Finance and Urban Affairs, US House of Representatives, 12 July.

Leutwiler, F. (1978), *Swiss Monetary and Exchange Rate Policy in an Inflationary World* (Washington, D.C.: American Enterprise Institute), p. 14.

McKinnon, R. I. (1977), *The Eurocurrency Market*, Essays in International Finance, No. 125, December (Princeton: International Finance Section, Princeton University).

Miller, William G. (1979), *Proposals to Facilitate the Implementation of Monetary Policy and to Promote Competitive Equality Among Depository Institutions*; Statement before the Committee on Banking, Housing and Urban Affairs, US Senate, 26 February.

Penner, R. G. and Silber, W. L. (1973), 'The interaction between federal credit programs and the impact on the allocation of credit', *American Economic Review*, vol. 63, pp. 838–52.

Solomon, A. M. (1979), *Statement*, Joint Hearing of Subcommittees of the Committee on Banking, Finance and Urban Affairs, US House of Representatives, 12 July.

Wallich, H. (1978), 'International lending and the Euro-markets', 1978 Euromarkets Conference sponsored by the Financial Times, London, 9 May.

Wallich, H. (1979), *Statement*, Joint Hearing of Sub-Committees of the Committee on Banking, Finance and Urban Affairs, US House of Representatives, 12 July.

7 Prognosis and Prescription

(i) *What of the Future?*

It is never possible to predict the economic future except by accident. It is often possible however to be sure that things will not go on as they are.

The simplest way to see that the Eurodollar market cannot continue to exist in its present form indefinitely is to put the question, 'Can any country stay *for ever* in deficit on its balance of payments?' The answer to this must be a qualified 'no'.

If a country is in permanent payments deficit its international debt must be growing continuously. The annual interest charge on that debt must therefore be growing and will for ever increase until, in due course, the sum to be paid abroad each year actually exceeds the whole of the gross national product of the debtor.

This is clearly a contradiction. Long before the event occurs both debtor and creditor will have perceived the necessity to call a halt to the process. And if a country cannot any longer borrow it cannot any longer continue in payments deficit. We do not know where the line will be drawn or how, but we do know that there must be some upper limit to the debt service charge due from any country, expressed as a proportion of its gross national product. There must therefore be some upper limit to the debt itself.

It is not necessary even to consider the ways in which a debt service charge might be settled. For present purposes we need only observe that, even on the most favorable assumptions for Eurodollar market growth, international debt cannot in the long run expand any faster than the money gross national product of debtor countries measured in the currency *least* subject to depreciation.

This last point is important. It is natural to suppose that

lenders will, as they gain experience, specify repayment in the most stable currency. As soon as debt becomes designated in a currency of even moderately stable purchasing power, no country which has reached the limit of its borrowing capacity in real terms can borrow further. It is true of course that as long as debt is designated in a depreciating currency it is automatically annihilated in real terms year by year at a rate equal to the rate at which the currency specified is losing its value. In such a case borrowing, even in real terms, can continue without violating the fixed real debt to real gross national product ratio. But all that is needed to eliminate this possibility is just one currency with a stable value. Such a currency must, in due course, come to be the unit of debt measurement, and when it does the practice of servicing debt by writing it off must come to an end. The rate of growth of total outstanding international debt, in money terms, will have to be reduced from its present 25 percent per annum to something like 2 percent, and even this would be most remarkable, for reasons now to be given.

Recall that we are living in very unusual times. Currency inflation is a common enough affair historically speaking but *never before* have we observed *all* currencies of the world losing value simultaneously at any significant rate. Such a phenomenon cannot continue.

Inflation always generates a learning process. Contracts come to be made, after a while, in terms which take into account the expected rate of inflation. This usually leads to still greater inflation which in the end forces traders to look for some other standard of value than the depreciating currency. The Weimar Republic in 1923 turned to the US dollar and thence to a 'New Mark'. Israel today both saves and sets prices in US dollars and other foreign currency units, not because dollars represent a fully satisfactory standard but because they represent a much better standard than the Israeli pound or sheckel. It will not be long before the world comes to recognize anew that it is no more possible to conduct affairs without a proper standard of value than it would be to conduct affairs without an agreed unit of length or weight. Proposals of many different kinds for a 'new' money are already under consideration and, since necessity is the mother of invention, we can be sure that in a historical perspective we do not have long to wait.

In parenthesis, it is worth reflecting on the fact that there is a considerable short-term profit awaiting the government with sufficient skill and courage to be the first to bring back proper money. As soon as the usefulness of the new currency is proven there will be an immediate international demand for it as the only satisfactory vehicle for trade, local or international. If the government concerned is as well informed as it will have proved itself to be by inventing the new money in the first place, it will not refuse to meet the market demand for the product of its ingenuity as, for example, the Swiss, and to some extent the West Germans, have in the past. On the contrary it will sell for foreign currency as much of the new 'valuable' money as may be called for, using the foreign money so acquired to buy land or other durable earning assets as appropriate throughout the rest of the world. This will hold exchange rates at the level required to maintain international purchasing power parity and at the same time reward initiative with a rate of return, while it lasts, on the, perhaps astronomical, amount of the new money supplied. When the rest of the world comes to its senses and presents for redemption any 'good' money it has held for speculative purposes this can be 'repurchased' (with the real foreign assets against which it was issued) and destroyed, again with no disturbance to exchange rates. Any good money which continues to be used internationally to support trade will go on providing a return through the real assets acquired by its sale, to the advantage of the issuing government.

Coming back now to the main theme suppose that inflation in terms of at least one currency has ceased and the limit to further international borrowing by debtor countries has been reached. Clearly the supply of funds to the Eurodollar market, by now the Euro-proper-money market, will have come to an end. Participating banks will be left with nothing to do except roll over existing loans and debts, albeit with a comfortable income. On the other hand can even the comfortable income continue?

In the first place the mere cessation of new borrowing must of itself have brought about a dramatic change in the pattern of world trade. Indeed, by definition, as long as former surplus countries continue to avoid deficits international payments and trade would have to be in balance. And then if any country, formerly in surplus, chose, for whatever reason, to spend some of its accumulated reserves either at home or abroad, at least one country would, by that act, be forced into corresponding surplus. But this would in no circumstances channel new funds into the Euro-proper-money market and might well take some out. If the country in trade surplus had been a net debtor to participating banks its proper-money earnings would simply go to reduce that debt. The Euromarket must shrink and with it the earnings real and nominal of participating banks. And even if the country in trade surplus was a net depositor there would be no upward change in total Euro-deposits; for the new deposits would be exactly matched by the withdrawal of funds by the country newly in deficit. The Euromarket must eventually reach a point where the only direction it can move is downward.

Furthermore the new discipline induced by the existence of a reliable accounting unit will encourage countries to view their overall position in a more rational light. Except in extra-ordinary circumstances it does not make sense for a country to create real capital overseas. In the first place there is a much greater risk of loss by debt repudiation, by currency de-preciation, or by some other cause deriving from the weak position of a creditor without rights of citizenship. But far more important than this is the very heavy social, as opposed to private, cost of foreign lending. What makes a country wealthy is its capital stock. The cost of acquiring capital is no greater when it is located at home than when it is located abroad. But total earnings at home are usually much greater. Capital raises the productivity of labor. From a purely selfish point of view it is better to raise the productivity of labor at home than abroad even when the rate of return on money capital is the same in both places. And in normal times the real rate of return is greater at home when due allowance is made for risk. The present situation is quite extraordinary.

In the world in which we currently live all the old rules of the game are in suspension. In a period of rapid inflation lenders lose in real terms more than they gain in interest. It becomes more important to invest in a stable currency than to earn an income from real capital. International bankers, apparently guaranteeing the eventual repayment of loans in a hard currency as well as a rate of return, look like a better bet than home investment in a currency rapidly depreciating in value. Furthermore inflation reduces the logic of taxation to the ridiculous by requiring lenders to pay when they incur real losses and allowing borrowers rebates when they make real gains. It becomes, so it would seem, profitable to be resident in one country while earning one's living in another.

Much more important is the fact, noted in Chapter 2 above, that the printing of money is of itself a prime cause of trade imbalances. When the current frantic round of money printing ceases, as it must, so will 'involuntary' capital lending. In a rational world with a restored 'automatic' balance of payments mechanism and greater stability in exchange rates there will be less need or desire for foreign exchange 'reserves' and a very much smaller supply of 'flight' capital invested abroad.

It is true of course that the world as a whole might quite properly wish to send foreign aid to less developed countries. But it will no longer be able to do this by 'lending' funds representing involuntary surpluses earned by countries who, if they had any say, or clearly understood what was being done to them, would have no wish either to accumulate surpluses or to lend their surpluses to less developed countries if they did.

Aid to LDCs will have to take the form of government face

to face loans, or the issue of special long-term bonds, or out-right gifts. In none of these cases is it either necessary or advisable to involve a private banking system.

(ii)　*Atrophy?*

For all of the reasons given above and more, it seems likely that the Eurodollar market in its present form will in due course begin to wither away. The flow of new funds will dry up. Whether or not there is a dramatic move to a new hard currency the rate of inflation will ultimately slow down, even though we may have to wait first to suffer harder lessons than we have to date. Existing real international debt will fall or be annihilated by inflation; or more of it will come to take the form of long-term government bonds issued directly by borrowing governments. Short-term monetary debt may also be repaid as presently debtor nations move into payments surplus following more responsible monetary behavior induced by belated recognition of the facts of life.

(iii)　*Or Dramatic Collapse?*

The alternative scenario is, of course, dramatic collapse and we have more than once referred to this possibility in the pages above. It should be made clear however that we ourselves do not expect a dramatic collapse in the popular sense even though it would be wrong to suppose that it could not happen. It is not true that we are moving inexorably towards a cata-clysmic financial crisis as writers of best sellers on the subject would sometimes have us believe (e.g. 'Adam Smith', 1981). Rather we see a financial crisis as something which can and should be prevented.

It is important to emphasize that, as long as deliberate fraud is ruled out, there is no reason why any properly organized financial arrangement should collapse. It is true that projects sometimes fail and bankruptcies ensue. But this is not unusual and the legal framework provides for such contingencies. Finance houses expect a proportion of bad debts and due allowance for them is made in their calculations.

Wholesale financial collapse however is quite another matter. On those occasions when a whole system has failed, or has seemed to fail, the fault is usually due to panic or misunderstanding. The special problem with the Eurodollar market is that it affords unusual scope for panic and misunderstanding on an international scale.

(iv) *Overhang?*

Perhaps the biggest misunderstanding of all is expressed by the word 'overhang'. The trillion dollars of Eurodebt is supposed to 'overhang' the US economy as if there were a possibility that one fine day the owners of that debt might appear and demand to buy, say, one half of the entire stock of private housing in the forty-eight continental states, currently valued at something like one trillion.

Of course nothing of the kind could happen. What is dangerous is not the possibility itself but the belief that such a possibility exists. The USA does not owe anyone one trillion dollars, nor has it issued that much money, nor has it received from foreigners a cumulative excess of imports over exports of more than one-tenth of 1 percent of the total world international debt. Paradoxically, however, the *belief* that the USA might be called upon to redeem a spectacular debt that is in reality none of its business could cause a panic and probably does already depress the value of the dollar below its purchasing power parity.

Paradoxically again, a panic could have precisely the opposite effect to that expected. The USA would be embarrased by a *demand* for dollars, not an excess supply of them. If Eurobanks were called upon to pay their creditors there would be a *shortage* of real dollars. Banks could then, in principle, fail because they have no dollars to pay; but they will not in practice. Almost certainly central banks would come to the rescue. Dollars would be printed and the panic averted. The danger is not that banks would fail but that the process of rescuing them would create huge sums of real money, most of which, once created, would never be destroyed again. The whole would be lent to someone, somewhere, to be spent since only this way can spending power earn income. A tidal wave of money, as always chasing too few goods, could raise prices, increase uncertainty and, in due course, fuel greater panics until, at last, out of necessity, cause and effect would come to be understood. The new stable money for which the world is waiting would have to be invented.

(v)   *Special Drawing Rights (SDRs) in Lieu of Overhang*

Fear of the dollar overhang has led to some curious proposals which could, if pursued, have precisely the consequences foreshadowed above, since they even more certainly imply the creation of new money to allay panic.

It has been suggested that some proportion of Eurodollar deposits should be converted to SDRs issued by the International Monetary Fund. What can this proposal mean? Perhaps it is intended that Eurobanks should be required to deposit a proportion, or initially the whole, of their flow of new dollars with the IMF rather than to onlend them to deficit countries. The IMF would then return the dollars to the USA by using them to buy US government bonds. This way, it is supposed, the dollar overhang, that is, dollars held by foreigners, would be returned to the country to which they belong. But would they be? If implemented the proposal would simply mean that foreign held deposits in US banks would have passed into the hands of the US citizens or institutions formerly owning the government bonds purchased by the IMF. What would those US institutional lenders now do with their newly acquired dollars? As likely as not they would redeposit them, directly or indirectly, in the Eurodollar market, which must, by the original act, be short of funds to meet the demands of deficit countries.

The dollar overhang would be in no way diminished. The

only consequence of the SDR proposal, if it is properly inter-preted above, would be to insert the IMF into the chain of 'banks' underwriting the loans of the surplus countries to those in deficit. If some Eurobank depositor wanted to withdraw dollars given up by his bank to the IMF for SDRs or any other IMF asset, and if the Eurobank had no dollars to pay, only SDRs, then no doubt the IMF would be obligated to 'cash' the bank's SDRs. In turn, the IMF would seek to cash its US government bonds for dollars not now in the hands of US institutions since they were onlent via Eurobanks to deficit countries. Almost certainly, then, the Federal Reserve System would be required to create new dollars to 'rescue' the IMF, and so on. Experience suggests that once created the new dollars would never disappear.

Other scenarios can be developed depending on alternative assumptions as to, not yet carefully specified, details of the scheme. All lead however to similar conclusions. Bank and/or IMF underwriting of debt on the scale presently existing promises what it cannot deliver, namely, liquidity, which does not exist. Promises in the end can (apparently) be kept only by influencing central banks to create new liquidity and with it inflation.

Changing names in no way alters cases. Furthermore the problem itself is not that which it is supposed to be. Banks underwriting debt can offer insurance against bad debt but their power to offer liquidity is strictly limited by the rate at which new funds are being deposited. Following the insurance principle bad debts can and should be paid for proportionately by all depositors. They should not be paid for by entire popu-lations by the creation of money unsupported by goods. Lack of liquidity is the price paid for the enjoyment of interest. Creditors should not expect both interest and liquidity, paid for by somebody else. The banking system must not claim to provide both interest and liquidity by relying upon the power of central banks (or the IMF) to create money, thereby forcing the whole community to share the cost through rising prices. Panic can cause a liquidity crisis but it does not cause bad debts. The chain of causation runs the opposite way. Those who fear the overhang fear bad debt without even knowing who is the debtor. The danger, if there is danger, lies only in the lack of liquidity at a time when nothing but panic is generating the demand for liquidity.

(vi)   *Repudiation of Debt*

As these words are being written, Poland, deeply in debt to Eurobanks, is about to have that debt 'rescheduled'.* This is of course sensible. No country wishes to repudiate unilaterally its debt if only because it thereby undermines its credit rating. Debt is a valuable saleable asset in the long run, and, so long as there is no panic, the owner of that debt can usually raise in cash whatever it is worth on world markets; and what it is worth depends mostly on the goodness or badness of the debt and scarcely at all upon liquidity.

The dangers of debt repudiation once again stem from misunderstanding. The misunderstanding is created partly by inflation and partly by Eurobanks themselves.

In times of inflation it is easy to borrow too much. The idea spreads that debt is a good thing since repayment can be made in depreciated currency. Unfortunately for borrowers, creditors get the message too. After a time lag interest rates rise in line with the inflation rate and the real burden of too much debt becomes intolerable.

At the same time inflation multiplies financial activity. The flow of funds increases and banks find it easier to borrow short term and lend long term. If and when the flow of new funds *slows*, sufficient liquidity can no longer be provided out of new deposits. Conditions are ripe for bad debts, panics and runs on the bank. If creditors understood that a reasonable proportion of bad debts are tolerable as long as they are shared, if banks made it clear to creditors at all times what their true liquidity

*More recently still the difficulties of Turkey, Sudan, Bolivia, Zaire, Jamaica and Peru, as well as Poland, have been a subject of comment (*The Economist*, 1981).

position was, and if arrangements existed to offer debt for sale at market price rather than to pretend a degree of liquidity which does not exist without central bank creation of paper money, there would be no problem.

The present writers believe that present international debt is not yet intolerable in a general way although it may become so if it continues to grow at its present rate. They believe also that if some bank debts do appear to be creating a crisis that crisis will be averted by international central bank support as in the case of Poland at present. In course of time the problem will come to be better understood and necessary reform of the system will be introduced.

To say this however is not to reject entirely the possibility of a major disaster such as that described above in the chronicles of Htrae (Chapter 3). Major bank failures, collapse of confidence, disastrous inflation, dramatic interference with international trade, unemployment on the scale of the 1930s, or complete disintegration of one or more major currencies are all real possibilities. But none of these events is inevitable. It is open to us now to make sure they do not occur.

(vii) *Prescription*

It is not the purpose of this section to propose a definite plan. There are many ways to achieve stability in international finance, all depending for their implementation on the degree of public understanding, the willingness of nations to co-operate, and the feasibility of inducing key financial institutions to change their methods. The necessary educational process cannot be separated from discussions which must surround the development of a detailed plan.

What is possible now, however, is to state the principles which all feasible plans must share. All must achieve certain basic and well-defined ends. These are set out below.

(1)   There must above all be a restoration of some automatic mechanism which will balance international trade and

payments. Nations must be taught through the operation of the market the necessity to consume only the value of what they produce, except as in (2) and (3) below. The mercantilist myth that trade surpluses are desirable or that stocks of foreign currency are necessary must be abandoned.

(2)   International lending, where it takes place, will permit spending in excess of the value of production but there must be a mechanism that will ensure that the lending nation saves what it lends. There must be an intended trade surplus corresponding to the borrowers' deficit. What is lent must be, ultimately, goods not money. Where the lending is underwritten by a financial institution it must be made clear that the service offered is insurance not liquidity. The financial instrument must be a long-term bond with the issuing bank's liability carefully defined.

(3)   Where international aid is offered it should again be ensured that what is given (or lent on favorable terms) is what has been saved by the giver. Giving away printed money unsecured by goods cheats everybody.

Principles (1), (2) and (3) above will bring to an end the current growth of Eurodebt as we know it. But it will not get rid of the existing stock of debt. This must be funded, that is, transformed into debt supported by a financial instrument such as that described in (2) above. Long-term international bonds should be marketable so that creditors may at any time secure the market value of the bond. In most cases of debt currently existing service charges could be met by the debtor so that there is no reason to expect impossibly large defaults. Creditors however should know what exactly it is that they own even if this should turn out to be something less than they thought they had deposited.

What appears above will at once be recognized as a council of perfection. Simply to state what we must have is sufficient to highlight the considerable political (but not technical) difficulty of achieving it. But the alternative is that international finance should become progressively more and more chaotic.

One further thing seems certain. It will be impossible to attain ends (1), (2) and (3) without the reintroduction, in some form, of proper money. Two principles must be satisfied for the new money to do what money is supposed to do.

(1) The unit of account must have an exact specified meaning in terms of value. As in the Middle Ages the price of goods must be the price of goods and not the inverse of the value of money as it is today. The dollar or the pound sterling must be defined in terms of goods and not by the meaningless promises currently inscribed upon them.

(2) The quantity of money in circulation must be determined, not by governments or banks in accordance with ill-specified theories scarcely capable of distinguishing money from debt, but by the market itself. Markets determine both the price and the quantity supplied of most goods. They should be allowed to do the same for money.

It is not difficult to secure both of these ends by more than one device. The introduction of the new money will solve no economic problem but it will at least show us what the problems are. Accountants will no longer need 'inflation accounting' for there will be no inflation.

We began this chapter, as we began the book, by asserting that the economic future is unpredictable. It is impossible to know when or how proper money will be reintroduced, but we know that it will. The Eurodollar phenomenon is no more than one facet of the multidimensional problem raised by the absence of a standard of value. Until this fact and other related facts are recognized our difficulties will multiply; and because they multiply we shall have no alternative but to recognize the truth in the end. A new money will appear and the nature of our financial institutions will change. The Eurodollar market will be seen as an historical incident, part horrifying and part funny. The attention of our successors will be diverted to some other apparent crisis, the logical consequence no doubt of whatever piece of conventional wisdom comes to be generated by our present inflationary and Eurodollar experiences.

Reference

'Adam Smith' (1981), *Paper Money* (New York: Summit Books).
The Economist (1981), April 4.

INDEX